# FROM THE GARDEN
# OF
# EDEN TO AMERICA

MW00736448

# FROM THE GARDEN OF EDEN TO AMERICA

BY AVANEDA D. HOBBS, Ed.D.

CSE BOOKS
P.O. Box 531403
Forestville, Maryland 20753

# HOBBS

# FROM THE GARDEN OF EDEN TO AMERICA

COPYRIGHT © 1997 HOBBS

ISBN 1-878898-04-3
Library of Congress Catalog No. 92-97508

Edited by:
  Royal Wendall Colbert, M.A., M.S.M., M.Div.

Printed in the U.S.A.
First Printing 1997

All correspondence and inquiries should be directed to:

CSE BOOKS
P.O. Box 531403
Forestville, Maryland 20753
(301) 499-0497 (Office)
(301) 499-8952 (Fax)

# SPECIAL THANKS

Special thanks are in order for Frederick and EmmaLisa Hobbs and family, the Dixon family, the entire family on my mom and dad's side, Nellie "Aunt Pal" Ceasar (the epitome of being absolutely wonderful), Evangelist Laura Hobbs and family, Prince Yelder, Towanda Spencer, Francina Sansbury, Lorraine Matterson, Lillian Maclin, Ellen "Wonderfully Gracious" Sanders, and Dr. Catherine McKinney. My personal prayers and best wishes are that God would prosper you beyond all that you could ask or think.

Special thanks and all my love to my pastors, Rev. Dr. Harry and Michelle Jackson of Hope Christian Center Church in College Park, Maryland. I am deeply grateful for the powerful teachings, awesome praise and worship, love and helping "this girl" to be all that I can be to the glory of God. We indeed are the light of the world, and wonderful instruments of God's glory and power to bring hope to the lost and to the hurting.

Heartfelt thanks, one million times over and some, to Pastor Crosby and Rose Bonner of the Alexandria Christian Center Church. I am so grateful to you and the ACC church family for allowing me to give birth to the "seed of reversal." Your vision and church are destined for absolute greatness.

Also, special thanks to Marcella Drula and the staff at Spectrum Publishing in Fairfax, Virginia. You have always come through for me, with the most magnificent artwork anyone could produce in this world . . . many, many thanks.

# DEDICATION

This book is lovingly dedicated to the memory of my father, Reverend Frederick Douglass Hobbs (1926-1987). I am eternally grateful to him for teaching me how to live holy and to depend on God for everything. More important, I willingly accept the apostolic and prophetic mantel he transferred to me 28 hours before leaving this earth. The same words prophetically spoken over his life were spoken over mine early that Sunday morning. Little did I know that Monday, February 23, 1987, would leave such an indelible impression . . . I was born on the 23rd and he departed this life on the 23rd. Perhaps in the simplicity of the little things did God, Himself, mark my future with undeniable clarity of purpose.

Mommy, I take this time to dedicate this work to you likewise. In my eyes you are the epitome of love. A woman of grace and elegance, you capture my attention and my desire is to be just like you. Your support over the years has been full of heart and commitment. You have spent countless hours and days just being there for me. You did it just so that I would know everything was going to be all right and that I was just to "go for it." Mom, you've brought me so much joy and I absolutely adore you. In case you didn't know, you are special to God and me, and to say so is still an understatement. I just wanted you to know that I love you dearly.

This book is also dedicated to Rev. Agnes Carter of Alexandria, Virginia. On the grounds of Woodlawn United Methodist Church, some 21 years ago, Agnes Carter gave me the first prophetic word I'd ever received. Those words set in course the beginnings of God's purpose and meaning for my life. She said, "Avaneda, God has great things in store for you. God, Himself, says that you are by divine appointment." Thanks Agnes, you'll never know how often those words have given me so much hope and encouragement. May history and mankind experience life and a change through me because of your obedience and love . . . enjoy the harvest with me.

Last, but certainly not least, is a dedication of this work to Oprah Winfrey. Once in a lifetime does the Creator bring such a gift to touch so many lives with love, candor and grace. While I was facing disappointments and a bad car accident that left me unable to walk for five months, I watched your show and saw how you overcame some personal dilemmas. You spoke words that have also helped to change my life's destiny. Oprah, you said, "it's all about truth." Just like the prophetic words spoken by Agnes Carter to me in 1976, so were those words. Although excruciatingly painful, it was truth that dug into festering wounds to bring a glorious healing to my entire being. With a new attitude and determination, I have conquered some insurmountable odds. I believe in myself and know that with God's help I can achieve the impossible. It is indeed all about truth. Thanks Oprah.

# PREFACE

The Body of Christ has been inundated with a spirit of religion. This spirit has illegally infiltrated the Church and is causing a stalemate between us and the goals God has mandated for us. satan has unleased the demon of the spirit of religion to seed the mentality of believers. This, in turn, can destroy the church and hinder the harvest of souls. In addition, the spirit of religion strives to slow down the return of Jesus Christ. The spirit of religion is defined as a spirit of complacency or a force that makes us relax and let our guards down.

The spirit of religion has given satan free course to deceive, manipulate the thinking and control the actions of many believers. We have even highly esteemed satan as having as much or greater power than us. Further, our Christian leaders have become weak, intimidated and defensive, instead of acting offensively.

The Church has not been using its God-given authority to run the devil off. Instead, it has courted church pettiness and traditional foolishness. The Church has become so preoccupied with religious foolishness that its leaders have abandoned their real purpose and call. As a result, predominantly black cities have the highest rates of illegitimate births, illiteracy, poverty and crime in the United States.

Our youths display a plethora of gifts, but are undisciplined and functionally illiterate. Ninety-eight percent of them are sexually active and abortions are at an all time high. Excellence has been replaced with satisfaction and it is having a debilitating effect on our people.

The reason for an immoral city is a weak and a scared church. A city without God and Godly people is weak. Our present leadership has allowed these situations to run rampid. The results for such actions are an uncontrolled society. It is visible everywhere. Regardless of what has transpired, God still loves us and wants to deliver His people out of bondage.

Christians are the interpretation of Jesus Christ, His ministry, His crucifixion and the fruitfulness of christian living in visible examples. Christians are the light of the world and a city that cannot be hidden (Matthew 5:14). They are also the body possessors of the awesomeness of the Godhead.

Our authority in knowing who we are in Jesus Christ determines our success in ruling and reigning here on earth. Because of this, Christians are to exemplify wisdom, control and exude love. Christians are also to be committed to excellence in the ministry of the gospel in reaching the world for Jesus Christ.

God honors us as His created beings. His desire is that we enjoy the cyclical experience of the love and warmth of His presence. God wants us to delight in the magnificence of His delivering power. He even gets pleasure when we rejoice in the omnipotence of His being.

II Corinthians 10:4 testifies of and summarizes the confidence and security we are to feel as Christians, when proceeding forward as God's witnesses to change the world.

> For the **weapons of our warfare**
> (God's Word and Power) are not of
> the flesh, but **divinely powerful** for
> the **destruction** of fortresses. (New
> American Standard Bible)

In these last days and times, the Spirit of God is moving to prepare us for His coming. The Bible's prophetic account of what is to take place before Jesus returns is being fulfilled today. We have seen many supernatural manifestations and are unable to deny that God is still in control. For example, the world witnessed the Soviet Union open its doors to born-again Christians to share the gospel of Jesus Christ with their citizens.

Prayer and consecrated living of Christians will provoke God to halt satan's control over our country. As Christians, we must submit and commit to righteousness. This will allow God to usher in His glory and to deliver our society out of its present dilemma.

Ephesians 5:27 states that God is returning for a "Church without a spot and a wrinkle." The Church's persecution has been severe. However, the shaking is not over. God loves us and is purifying and purging us with fire, to present us faultless and blameless before Him when He returns.

With Christ's return in mind, I felt an urgency to compile a book that could be used to promote awareness, union and unity. Thus, From The Garden of Eden to America, The Guide To Black Religious and Supporting Organizations was borne. This book is a comprehensive guide that provides information on the scriptural history of the black man. It offers a definitive analysis and prognosis of the black church and the plight of the black man and his religion.

An indepth study was also conducted on the denomations that exist in America and how they originated. Finally, a comprehensive model has been developed to begin a project of tracking black church denominations, ecumenical organizations and service agencies in any geographical location. The Washington, D.C. area was used in the sampling, to create a systematic methodology for others to use.

It is my hope that this will enhance interactions with other churches and ministries not in one's immediate denomination. I also want to provoke the thinking of those "religious persons" to answer the question, "am I promoting Jesus Christ, harmony or discord among the brethren?"

# TABLE OF CONTENTS

x

# SECTION I

# A BIBLICAL PERSPECTIVE OF THE BLACK MAN, HIS RELIGION AND HIS CHURCH

# CHAPTER 1
## *WHO AND WHAT IS BLACK?*

The earth was without form and void until God spoke and it became filled with substance and living beings. When God saw that all was good He wanted fellowship. God wanted communion with someone who could rule His creation. God did not want communion with animals, but someone like Himself. In the Garden of Eden, God formed Adam from the dust of the ground, and Adam became a living soul.

The correlation between the definitive references of Adam's name to the Garden of Eden coincides with the word human. The Hebrew noun 'ādām in its general sense denotes "*human being*" and "*human kind.*" It also occurs as the proper name of the first of the forefathers of the human family in I Chronicles 1:1. Ādăm can also be defined as "*of the ground or taken out of red earth.*" Etymologists denote the prefix of human, hu, to mean person of color. Thus, the original Hebrew definition for Adam has two meanings. First, it describes Adam as a human being. Second, it interprets Adam's name to mean the ground ('adhāmāh) or in more definitive terms, his soul's origin.

The verb rendered "*formed*" in the Old Testament speaks of a potter molding clay. Ne´phesh, meaning soul, refers to a complete or whole person.

The Garden of Eden is referred to, in Sumerian terms, as a lush fertile plain. Genesis describes the Garden of Eden as a tropical place undergirded by a river. Further, it describes a "mist" that rose from the earth and watered the ground in the Garden of Eden. The mist was a natural resource.

When combined with water, particularly in the Garden of Eden, dust creates a colored mixture. This mixture is most commonly called red earth. For instance, ancient Greeks frequently spoke of Adam or Africans as red Negroes with copper-tone colored skin.

We can draw the following conclusions from the above by stating the following. First, Adam's body was made in the Garden of Eden. Second, Adam came out of the dust of the ground. Third, dust was mixed to form Adam's body from a mist that rose up from the earth. Fourth, the first man produced from the ground and from the Garden of Eden was a person of color. Genesis 2:7, thus, can now read:

> *In the Garden of Eden, Yahweh-Elohim*
> *(God) the potter molded from clay (formed)*
> *a reddish copper-tone human being (Adam)*

*from the dust of the ground . . . and human
kind (man) became a living and complete
person (soul).*

Scientific researchers indicate in their reports that man is a unique species. Many professionals in the field of anthropology have dedicated their lives to the study of the evolution of the original man. They state that man came from one source of being, as well as the premise that all of humanity or mankind began in Africa. These professionals have preserved fossils and the remains of Blacks who lived several thousand years ago. Their studies support the premise that mankind is a descendant of the African. Specifically, they show that the primary differences in mankind can be found only in skin color or pigmentation. This, they say, is evident and can be seen in the various races.

Other research studies have focussed on the syllogism that mankind is the sole survivor of the African. These studies further surmise that the African has peopled the universe over the centuries. The oldest modern fossils of humans have been uncovered from Africa and are dated back approximately 10,000 years ago. One recent discovery includes the human remains of an African woman who is thought to be the first woman of mankind, Eve.

Leading genetic scientists indicate, with little opposition, that the woman carries a hereditary material that is genetically passed on to her offspring. This genetic material is transferred from mother-to-daughter. From generation-to-generation this material is transmitted and is mildly changed over the years of countless generations. The only woman to have had at least one daughter, in every generation from the beginning of mankind up to the present, is Eve.

Genetic scientists have substantiated and documented through their studies that the gene transmitted through the woman is found in *ALL* humans. Despite some theorists' disbelief in the Garden of Eden, this discovery infallibly substantiates that all peoples originated from the Garden of Eden. It also points to the Garden of Eden, the place where God created mankind as an African. Adam, created in God's image and molded from the dust of the ground, is the original person from which mankind emanates.

Other conclusive evidence that has been entered into record includes the transcriptions of European anthropologists. Their information states that the fossil remains of an African man revealed that his body structure was the only kind that could've survived in Eden's tropical climates. This assumes that they actually knew the location of Eden. In addition, these anthropologists believe that the texture of the African's skin was the only type that could've survived in Eden's environments.

Mankind did not originate from apes or monkeys. The evidence presented clearly eradicates this erroneous theory. The primary deduction that does away with this theory is that mankind cannot interbreed with animals. Moreover, animals cannot interbreed with humans because the substance or DNA that would make them human is not present.

## CHAPTER 2
# *THE GEOGRAPHICAL SIGNIFICANCE OF THE GARDEN OF EDEN*

Where did the earth begin? What are its territories? The beginnings of territories that influenced the world's population expansion and the people responsible for its implementation are explored in this section.

The Garden of Eden is the most significant place on earth. It holds within its borders the origin of mankind and the progression of world development (Genesis 2:7,11-14). Genesis 2:10-14 records the territory of the Garden of Eden as being located in Cush or the northern region of Ethiopia, North Africa.

The land of Cush was once surrounded by four rivers that flowed into one to water the Garden of Eden (Genesis 2:13). The importance of these rivers is the territory it defines. Second, is how it supports the creation and gradual unfolding of mankind's history.

One river flowed from Cush into four separate rivers. Those four rivers, from the one river, were the Pishon, Gihon, Hiddekel and the Euphrates.

The Pishon River flowed from the land of Havilah. The Gihon or Nile River flowed from the land of Cush. The Hiddekel or Tigris River flowed from east of Assyria. The Euphrates River flowed from southwest Asia. Figure 1, on the next page, helps you to visualize this description.

Some theologians present the four rivers as those encircling the entire earth. The Pishon is said to encircle Arabia and flows into the Nile. The Nile, in turn, rises with the Euphrates, crosses below the Persian Gulf and encircles Ethiopia. This theory presupposes that Africa and India were connected when the Arabian and Persian Gulfs were considered to be lakes.

## The Pishon River

The Pishon and Gihon Rivers are almost always mentioned simultaneously. Both rivers run east as far as the Inus and southwest to Africa's Nile. The Pishon River is only mentioned once in the Bible. The Gihon River, however, is mentioned again as a spring east of Jerusalem.

## The Land Of Havilah

The location of Havilah is known from a Sabean inscription. The inscrip-tion says that Havilah is located north of Yemen as a region named Haulan. Haulan is the territory surrounded by the Pishon branch of Eden's river in North Sheba,

17

# FIGURE 1
## THE RIVERS AND TERRITORIES
## SURROUNDING THE GARDEN OF EDEN

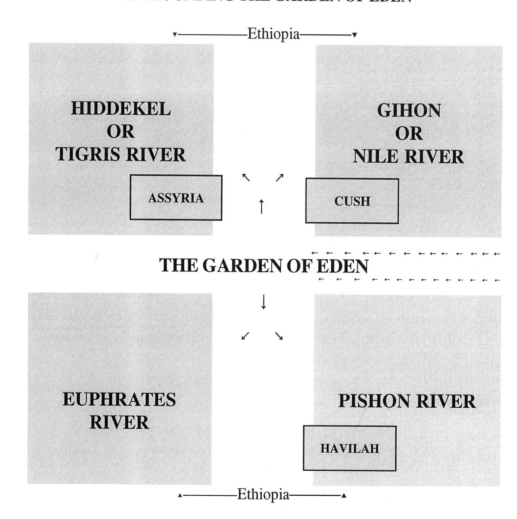

Saudi Arabia. Havilah also lies on the border of the land by Ishmael's descendants. Havilah is identified with sand and understood merely as a description for the "land of sand."

The inhabitants of Havilah were descendants of Cush and the offspring of Eber's son, Joktan. Eber is the ancestor of thirteen old-Arabian tribes and a link between Hebrew and Arabian stocks.

## The Gihon or Nile River

The appellative from the root of Gihon means to "burst forth." Gihon is the popular spring east of Jerusalem. It surrounds what is now known as Jerusalem and was once its main source of water supply.

## The Land Of Cush

Cush (Kush) or Ethiopia is the oldest independent country in the world. It is the legendary ancient region of northeast Africa called Ethiopia. Cush borders on Egypt and is surrounded by the Gihon or Nile River.

Ethiopia is located on the eastern horn of Africa and is bound on the north by the Red Sea and the French territory of the Afars and Issas. On the east, it is bound by the Somali Democratic Republic. Kenya is on the south of Ethiopia and Sudan is on the west. Cush was established by a son of Ham and entered into history accordingly.

# The Hiddekel or Tigris River

Hiddekel is the Hebrew name for the Tigris River. The Tigris River flows toward the east of Assyria and frames the region of Mesopotamia. It is comprised of Assyria on the north and Babylon on the south.

Today, the Tigris River runs through the heart of Iraq and flows into the Persian Gulf. It is important to note that the Euphrates River runs parallel to the Tigris River.

## The Land Of Assyria

Assyria was built on the western bank of the Tigris River. Assyria also extends from north Babylon to the country west of the Euphrates River. Today, Assyria lies within the borders of Iraq. It occupies the alluvial region between the Euphrates and Tigris Rivers, from Baghdad south to the Persian Gulf.

## The Euphrates River

The Euphrates River, once called the "good and abounding great river" according to Old Testament writings, is the longest river in southwest Asia. Early records show that both the Tigris and Euphrates Rivers entered into the Persian Gulf. At a large canal, it showed that the Euphrates River left above Babylon and ran east to the Tigris River.

The Euphrates River measures 780 miles and has upper, middle and lower divisions. The upper division of the Euphrates is formed by the Frat and Murad branches, northeast of Mt. Ararat. The middle section of the Euphrates extends for approximately 700 miles and forms the long-recorded boundary between the Assyrians and the Hittites. The lower part begins 100 miles above Babylon and 50 miles below where the Tigris and the Euphrates Rivers are approximately 25 miles apart.

# CHAPTER 3
# *THE BEGINNING OF A*
# *NEW GENERATION*

## Noah - The Second Father of Mankind

Adam was God's first created being. Adam's treason against the God who created him plunged mankind into apostasy.

Treason or apostasy is defined as **SIN**. Sin, or the wrong nature, infiltrated the spirits and souls of humans. Sin forced mankind to become wicked creatures and idol worshippers. God's attitude was to eradicate sin.

Lamech named his son Noah to reflect a new hope for the people who were to hear his name. Every time the people heard the name Noah, they heard "Yahweh has cursed the ground but this child shall bring us relief."

The reformation of the origin of mankind began with Noah. He is called the first tiller of the soil or "man of the ground." Noah's birth was the first after Adam's death of 126 years. Noah, the second father of mankind and ninth in descent from Adam, assumed this title after the Great Flood. The Great Flood destroyed everyone on the face of the earth except Noah and his family. Their lives were spared because of Noah's obedience to God.

Noah had an intimate relationship with God and knew what commitment God required of mankind. His obedience to God's commands proved worthwhile, as he and his entire family were spared from extinction or eradication.

God instructed Noah, a blameless and righteous man, to begin building an ark 120 years before the Great Flood. Per God's instructions, Noah built the ark in Mesopotamia. This ark was to hold his immediate family and one of each male and female species that had been made at that present time.

While Noah was building the ark, he prophesied to the people about a flood that was coming to destroy a wicked nation. No one listened. Instead, they mocked and scorned him.

When God's instructions had been fulfilled and the ark was completed, it began to rain. For forty days and forty nights it rained vehemently. The Great Flood that had been prophesied came and destroyed every living being who did not enter the ark. After the rain subsided, the ark landed on Mount Ararat or what is better known as Armenia. There, Noah's descendants began spreading all over the earth.

Mankind was redeveloped from Noah's three sons. They were Shem (Israelites), Ham (Canaanites) and Japheth (Philistines). Shem was the ancestor of the Hebrews, Arameans and Arabs. Ham was the ancestor of the Canaanites. Japheth was the ancestor of the Aryan or Indo-European peoples.

Noah's descendants migrated from the east to a plain in the land of Sumer. Sumer is located between the Tigris and the Euphrates Rivers. There, Noah formed the first civilization. Noah lived 350 years after the Flood, to the ripe old age of 950.

## A New World - A New Beginning

On the first day of 601 B.C. of Noah's life, he removed the covering of the ark. Noah looked and beheld that the surface of the ground was dry from the Great Flood. On the 27th day of the second month of 601 B.C., the earth was completely dry.

God then spoke to Noah and told him to take all of his family and every living creature from the ark and begin replenishing the earth. Noah obeyed God's instructions. First, Noah built an altar to God, took one of every clean animal and bird and offered burnt offerings to the Lord. The aroma of the sacrifice was so soothing that God, Himself, promised never to curse the ground on the account of man. God said that the intent of man's heart from his youth would always be evil.

Noah began farming the earth and planted a vineyard for his family. One day at the end of his labor, Noah relaxed and began drinking wine from the crop he had cultivated. He became intoxicated and completely disrobed himself in his tent.

Ham, Noah's youngest son, saw his father's nakedness. Ham went and told his two brothers what he had seen. Shem and Japheth, startled at the news, took a garment and laid it upon both of their shoulders. They walked backwards inside the tent to cover their father's nakedness. Shem and Japheth made sure that their faces were turned away from seeing Noah's nude body.

When Noah awoke from his drunken stupor he knew what Ham had done. Noah reprimanded Ham by placing a curse on Canaan's succeeding generations. He prophesied that Canaan's descendants would have a servants' role to his brothers.

Noah's prophecy states that the descendants of Japheth (Aryans) and Shem (Shemites) would get along with each other. The highly cultured Hamites (Canaanites), however, would be servants to Shem and Japheth. The curse recorded in Genesis 9:27 says:

> *Cursed be Canaan; a servant of*
> *servants shall he be to his brethren.*
> *Blessed be the Lord God of Shem;*
> *and Canaan shall be his servant.*
> *God shall enlarge Japheth, and he*

*shall dwell in the tents of Shem; and*
*Canaan shall be his servant.*

This is the first record of slavery that is recorded in the Hebrew Bible. The objective of slavery for the Hamitic servants' role to his brothers was to bring the Black man out of apostasy and arrogance. It was to place Blacks where they would serve God with humility.

## The Table Of Nations

The ethnological line for Noah, as mentioned in Genesis 10, is set forth in Figure 2 on the next page. The Old Testament ethno-linguistic table of Bible lands, described in Genesis 10, is presented in Figure 3.

## FIGURE 3
### Old Testament Ethno-Linguistic Table

| Shem (Semitic) | Ham (Hamitic) | Japheth (Indo-European) |
|---|---|---|
| 1. Akkadians | 1. Sumerians | 1. Hitties |
| 2. Amorites | 2. Canaanites | 2. Indo-Aryans |
| 3. Arameans | 3. Elamites | 3. Philistines |
| 4. Arabic | 4. Kassites | |
| | 5. Hurrians | |
| | 6. Anatolians | |
| | 7. Egyptians | |
| | 8. Cushites | |

# FIGURE 2
## The Ethnological Breakdown Of Noah

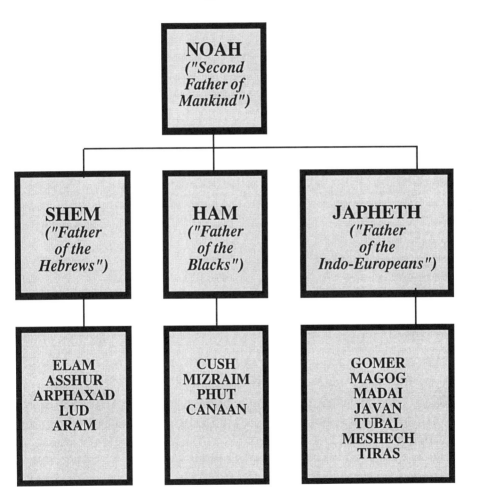

# SHEM

The beginning of Noah's prophesy started with his oldest son, *Shem*. Shem's loyalty to His father was rewarded by Noah's promise that the worship of the true God would continue among his descendants. Shem, whose name means renown, is the ancestor of the Hebrews, Arameans, Arabs or Semites, and the Semitic language and religion.

Shem, the dark or dusky complexioned son, settled his descendants between Ham and Japheth. The Shemites settled in the country that had Ancient monumental statutes, which was used to verify and track the development of the Shemitic races. From these monuments, it is now factual proof that many Hamitic people populated Europe, Asia, Africa and South Arabia. The Hamites prepared the way for the Hebrew or Shemitic race.

The Hebrew people were members or descendants of a northern Semitic people, better known as the Israelites. Jews are descendants of the Hebrew people and are also known as descendants of the Semites.

The Shemitic religion evolved around monotheism (believe in one God), totemism (ancestor worship) and polydaemonism (animal sacrifice). Shem's sons, Elam, Assur and Arphaxad, helped him form this ancestry. The figure on the following page delineates the ethnological and geographical structure for Shem and his descendants.

## FIGURE 4
### The Ethnological And Geographical Breakdown
### Of The Sons Of Shem

| SHEM ("Father") | |
|---|---|
| *Ethnological* | *Geographical* |
| ELAM | Assyria (S.W.) |
| ASSHUR | Assyria |
| ARPHAXAD | North Assyria |
| LUD[1/] | W. Asia Minor |
| ARAM | Syria |

[1/] Lud or Ludim's descendants are intertwined with Mizraim (Cush).

# Elam

*Elam* and his ancestors, branded as wild plundering people, were known to be skillful users of the bow and arrow. The Elamite people were very idolatrous. Their idolatry was carried over as they established territorial lands from the Persian Gulf to Assyria on the north. Idolatry was even prevalent from the Zagros mountains on the east and the Tigris on the west. The Elamites also populated the capital of Shushan, known as a powerful and magnificent city of antiquity.

# Asshur

*Asshur*, Shem's second son, was the god to whom the Assyrian people lifted their prayers to for help. Asshur was known as a deity and a protector of the Assyrian people. The Assyrian people were comprised of Semitic and Hurrian (Horites) elements. The significance of this group of people was their use by God as scourges to punish apostasy. An art object in the form of a sun dial, with an archer shooting a shaft, was left as a memorial to Asshur.

# Arphaxad

*Arphaxad*'s third son, who was born two years after the Great Flood, is considered to be important in priestly genealogy. Arphaxad, tenth in the family line, is the link between Shem and Abraham. He was king of the Medes, reigned in Echbatana and was defeated and killed by Nebuchadrezzar.

30

# Lud

*Lud* was the first born of Mizraim and the fourth son of Shem. Lud is the father of the Lydians or Luden people. The Luden people originally settled north of Palestine and afterwards in Asia Minor.

Though it is recorded that Lud was the father of the Lydians, the Lydians were not 100% Shemites. The Lydians were co-descendants of Mizraim. Lud's descendants were recognized as excellent archers who were employed in the Egyptian and Tyrian armies.

## Aram

*Aram*, Shem's youngest son, formed the Aramean descendants. Arameans are identified as Syrians, whose geographic territory is Syria. The Greek word for the region of Syria is never used in the Hebrew as Syria but always as Aram. Arameans were also a group of people who lived between the Taurus Mountains, the region of Damascus and from Lebanon to east of the Euphrates.

# HAM

*Ham*'s Hebrew name means "to be hot." He is the second son of Noah and the father of the Canaanites. Ham's sons listed in Genesis 10 and I Chronicles 8 are Cush, Mizraim (Egypt), Put and Canaan. Ham represents the Black race. This race of people are recorded as dominating the first 2,000 years of world history.

The land of Ham connotes Egypt. It is regarded as the original ancestor of the Egyptian peoples. The land of Ham starts from Phoenicia through W. Palestine into Africa and West Africa.

Hamites are members of a group of related people who inhabited northern and northeastern Africa. They include the Berbers and descendants of ancient Egyptians. Also included is a subfamily of the Hamites and the Coptic and Cushitic languages of Ethiopia. On the next three pages, Figures 5-7 show the ethnological and geographical structure for Ham and his descendants.

## Cush

*Cush*, the first son of Ham, was the father of Nimrod. Nimrod founded Babel and other states of Babylonia.

## Mizraim

*Mizraim*, the grandson of Noah, is the ancestor of Hamitic peoples. Some Hamitic people lived in lower Egypt and northwest of the Delta in Africa. Some Hamitic or Raaman peoples are from southwest Arabia.

Mizraim is the Hebrew name for Egypt. Mizraim or Egypt borders on the northeast corner of the African continent and is the most populous country

# FIGURE 5

## The Ethnological And Geographical Breakdown
## Of The Sons Of Ham

| HAM *(Father)* | | | |
|---|---|---|---|
| CUSH[1/] | MIZRAIM[1/] | PHUT[1/] | CANAAN[1/] |
| CUSH[2/] Ethiopia | MIZRAIM[2/] Egypt | PHUT[2/] Libya | CANAAN[2/] Palestine |
| S. Arabia[3/] N.Arabia Persian Gulf S.Egypt Sudan N.Ethiopia | N.Africa[4/] Crete S.Israel Palestine | Libya[4/] | Lebanon[4/] Rome Asia Minor China Jerusalem Judea Arka Sin-oriental Hama |

[1/]   Ethnological Sons of Ham.
[2/]   Geographical Sons of Ham.
[3/]   Original correlation for the geographical territory of the Sons of Ham.
[4/]   Modern day correlation for the geographical territory of the Sons of Ham.

# FIGURE 6
## The Ethnological And Geographical Breakdown
## Of The Grandsons Of Ham

| HAM (Father) | | | |
|---|---|---|---|
| **CUSH**[1/] | **MIZRAIM**[1/] | **PHUT**[1/] | **CANAAN**[1/] |
| Seba[2/]<br>Havilah<br>Sabtah<br>Raamah<br>Nimrod<br>Sabtecha | Ludim[2/]<br>Anamim<br>Lehabim<br>Naphtuhim<br>Pathrusim<br>Casluhim<br>Caphtorim | No One Listed[2/] | Sidon[2/]<br>Heth<br>Jebusites<br>Amorites<br>Girgasites<br>Hivites<br>Arkites<br>Sinites<br>Arvadites<br>Zemarites<br>Hamathites |
| Egypt[3/]<br>Abyssinia<br>S.W. Red Sea<br>Arabia<br>Chaldea<br>Ethiopia | W. Africa[3/]<br>Mareatis<br>Libya<br>Memphis<br>Thebos-Pathros<br>Arabia-Petra<br>Damieta | Libya[3/] | Sidon[3/]<br>Hitties<br>Jerusalem<br>Judea<br>Gergesenes<br>Shechem<br>Arke<br>Sinnas<br>Arvad<br>Sumrah<br>Hamath |

---

[1/] Ethnological Grandsons of Ham.
[2/] Geographical Grandsons of Ham.
[3/] A modern correlation for the geographical territory of the Grandsons of Ham.

34

# FIGURE 7
## The Ethnological And Geographical Breakdown
## Of The Great Grandsons of Ham

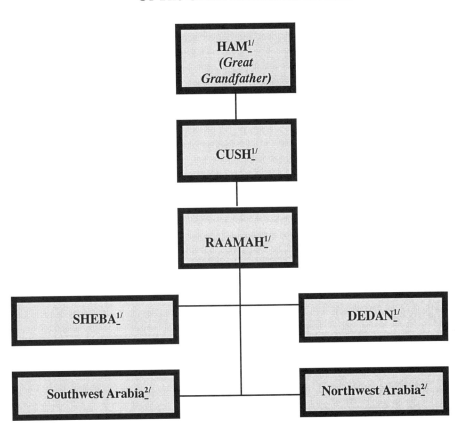

---

1/   The ethnological breakdown is as follows:  Great grandfather -- Ham; Grandfather --
Cush; Father -- Raamah; and the Sons -- Sheba and Dedan.

2/   The geographical Sons of Raamah.

in the Arab world. It is also the second most populous on the African continent. Egypt is bordered by the Mediterranean Sea, Libya, Sudan, Red Sea, the Gulf of Suez and the State of Israel. Egypt has the longest recorded history in the world.

## Put

*Put* or *Punt* (Somaliland) is better known as the region lying along the south end of the Red Sea. It is also known as the region along the west shore of the Indian Ocean.

"Put" is the region of East Africa including Somalia, Djibouti and eastern parts of Ethiopia. Djibouti is divided between Somalis, Afars and Dahkils.

Put, referred to with Ethiopia as the "horn of Africa," was inhabited by Cushitic peoples. This country is bounded on the north by the Gulf of Aden and east and south by the Indian Ocean. Put is also bounded on the west by the Afars, Issas, Ethiopia and Kenya.

Put and Djibouti are Hamitic peoples and nearly all are Muslims. This foreign community also included Greeks, Indians, Italians, Arabs and the French.

Many of the descendants of Put were known to mingle with Arab and Persian traders. These people formed the Somali culture, a primarily Muslim community in East Africa.

# Canaan

*Canaan* was the fourth and youngest son of Ham and the progenitor of the Phoenicians. Canaan was used to begin the suffering of Ham's shame and reproach to Noah. Noah's prophecy to Ham was that Canaan and his descendants would endure shameless profligacy and insufferable abominations.

Religiously speaking, the Canaanites were considered worshippers of the most hateful as the most holy. They were recognized as having been a part of some of the most heinous and idolatrous ceremonial rituals.

# JAPHETH

*Japheth* is the third son of Noah or the forbearer of Gomer, Magog, Madai, Javan, Tubal, Meshech and Tiras. To the Jewish people, Japheth's name in Hebrew refers to and means those people of non-Semitic and non-Hamitic origin, who were more white-skinned.

Japheth's descendants were better known as Indo-European or Indo-Iranian peoples. They were of the west highlands of Asia Minor and from the rugged plateau south of the Caspian Sea. Japheth's descendant also settled around the Black Sea, to the northeast shores and on the islands of the Mediterranean.

# FIGURE 8
## The Ethnological And Geographical Breakdown
## Of The Sons Of Japheth

| JAPHETH ("Father") | |
| --- | --- |
| *Ethnological* | *Geographical* |
| GOMER | Crimeria-Wales |
| MAGOG | Gyges-Asia Minor |
| MADAI | Indus |
| JAVAN[1] | Greece |
| TUBAL[1] | Greece |
| MESHECH | S.E. Asia Minor |
| TIRAS | Italy |

[1]   Javan and Tubal were known to have traded slaves.

# Gomer

*Gomer* was the oldest son of Japheth. He was the father of the Ammerians who inhabited Wales (Cambria) and Cumberland, England. The figure on the next page shows the ethnological and geographical structure for Japheth and his descendants. Gomer's descendants were considered as barbarian Lordes. They settled in what is now called southern Russia.

# Magog

The second son of Japheth was the founder of the Scythian descendants. They were a tribe that is now called Russian. The nation of *Magog* was located in the north near Togarnah and the maritime regions of Europe. Magog is sometimes called heathens and opponents of Messiah. Magog is also referred to as enemies of Israel.

# Madai

The third son of Japheth, *Madai*, is responsible for the Medes ancestors, language and religion. The Medes religion is closely allied with the Persians.

Madai's descendants were considered ancient Aryands (Iranians) and Indo-European peoples. These descendants invaded the territories south of the Caspian Sea. By 700 B.C., the Medes people had built the land of Javan upon a prosperous realm called Media.

# Javan

Japheth's fourth son, *Javan*, was the ancestor of the "coastland peoples" of the nations or isles of the Gentiles. Javan, the Hebrew for Greece or Greeks, was the father of Elishah. Elishah were the people of Hellas, Italy. Hellas is a region near Cicilia, Tarshish, Kittim (Cyprus) and Dodanim (Rodanim).

The significance of Javan and his descendants is to account for the origin of early island and coastland peoples. Javan's descendants were known to have traded slaves. (Many of these slaves were said to have come from Ghana.)

# Tubal

*Tubal* is the fifth son of Japheth and is referenced with his brother, Meshech. Both Tubal and Meschech were known to be exporters of slaves, copper and brass. Tubalans were also considered warlike people of antiquity.

# Meshech

*Meshech* and his descendants were regarded as remote and barbaric people. Meshech's descendants lived primarily about Armenia, southwest Asia Minor and west of his brother, Tubal. Meschech and his family ancestors were considered to be an enemy of the Assyrians.

Meschech is mentioned in Scripture as always being in the company of his brothers, Tubal and Javan. Ezekiel mentions, on several occasions, that Meshech and his brothers, Javan and Tubal, were traders of brass and slaves. In addition, Gog and Magog, Meshech's other brothers, were mentioned as being part of the underworld.

## Tiras

*Tiras*, seventh son of Japheth, was known as a race of Pelasgian pirates and seafaring peoples who invaded Egypt. Tiras has been associated with the Aegean Islands, Thrace, Tarsus and Tarshish, places where African slaves were traded.

# CHAPTER 4
## *DEFINING THE WORD CHURCH*

Before proceeding forward with a prognosis of the Black church, we must first define the word *church*. In this section, we will discover the origin, meaning and purpose for the church.

During the Roman Empire period, Greeks were acquainted with Jesus Christ through their intellect. They were recognized as extraordinary thinkers and philosophers. The strength of their reasoning and philosophical capabilities was their pursuit of wisdom and self-discipline. The Greeks' need to understand the underlying causes and laws of reality was foremost.

God used the Greeks' intellectual and philosophical abilities to implement rulership principles and concepts to govern the world's society. These concepts and principles were the development of a democracy for which the church was to be founded. In turn, they initiated the definitive meaning of the word church.

The word church was derived during the historical Roman Empire. The word church was also used by Greeks to describe a group of people selected by the Lord. Their job was to sit with the Lord and to get His mind. God's mind would then be put into laws to be obeyed by all mankind.

The following parable paints a picture of how God used the Greeks' skills to develop the church's meaning and role. In a parable made to His disciples in Matthew 16:18, Jesus said, *"Upon this rock I will build my church; and the gates of hell shall not prevail against it."* At the time Jesus made this parable, Caesar Augustus was ruler of the Roman Empire. The Greek renderence for the name Caesar meant lord. The inference here was a position of rulership not lordship over mankind. According to the Greek interpretation for Caesar, lords were to sit with God in a chamber or a secret place of prayer. There, God would talk His mind to them.

When God spoke, the lords wrote down everything they heard Him say. The lords took God's thoughts, translated them into legislation and turned the legislation into policy. These policies later became laws. Laws were then enacted throughout the whole empire. People, both near and in far provinces, became subject to the law and began adhering to the mind of the Lord. Greeks never considered the church as a religious body, but a political or diplomatic group chosen by God.

In conclusion, Jesus Christ's parable meant that upon Christ would a church or a group of legislators be constructed. Upon Christ's thoughts and ways, a group of legislators need not be afraid of demonic onslaughts. They could not prevail against anything built upon Jesus Christ.

God created a diplomatic chore of people who would maintain mankind's sovereignty and not be subject to demonic influences. Instead, hell and its forces would suffer violent spiritual attacks from God's diplomatic chore. In addition, satanic powers would always be anesthetized by God's people because they had been deputized to carry out God's commands with authority and power.

# CHAPTER 5
# *THE ORIGIN AND FOUNDATION OF BLACK AMERICA'S ORGANIZED RELIGION*

## Protestantism vs. Catholicism

Protestants have always been viewed as people who protest about something. Protestants may not have been sure of what they were for, but, they were very sure of what they were against.

To modern ears, the word protest carries a negative connotation. However, when all that has been acknowledged and documented, it is erroneous to describe Protestantism as "protest against." First, the word protest itself has a different meaning, a positive meaning. The word "to protest" comes from the Latin word *pro-testari* and means not only to testify, but, to testify on the behalf of something. Webster gives as a synonym, "to affirm." The Oxford English dictionary defines it as "to declare formally in public, to testify or to make a solemn declaration." To protest, then, in the true meaning of the word, is to make certain affirmations or to give testimony for something.

Second, the image of Protestantism fails to do justice to the interest of the Protestant Reformers. If the Reformers were against something, it was only because they were primarily for something.

Third, no faith lives by its denials. The denials are by-products of the affirmations. To believe in salvation by grace, for example, means opposing salvation by works, as it does today. By the same logic, to believe in racial integration means to oppose segregation. What's important here is that the negative consequence grows out of the positive affirmation and not vice versa.

Roman Catholics believe various matters constitute the fullness of the Christian faith. Protestants, on the other hand, believe fewer circumstances constitute the Christian faith. The image rests on a confusion over the meaning of the fullness of the faith. This is particularly true when it is related to the words "Catholic" and "Roman Catholic."

Roman Catholics believe in "all seven sacraments," while Protestants believe in only two. The fullness of the faith cannot be measurably defined. That is, having seven sacraments is not better than having two. In that case, having twelve would be better still. There is always the possibility that the observance of two sacraments represents the norm. The observance of more than two, however, could represent a departure from the norm. Confusion surrounds the use of the words Catholic and Roman Catholic.

The Roman Catholics feel confident that the words can be used interchangeably. For them catholicity or wholeness is found only in that branch of Christendom which acknowledges the bishop of Rome as the vicar of Christ. Protestants cannot accept this understanding of catholicity. They feel that at certain basic points Roman Catholicism departs from the Catholic faith rather than exemplifies it. The equation of Catholic and Roman Catholic must therefore be rejected by Protestants. The equation must also be rejected because with it comes the notion of Protestantism as diluted Catholicism.

Protestants with a conservative theological orientation often imply that to be a Protestant is to assent to a group of carefully defined doctrines. High on the list will be a claim about the Bible, usually couched for the doctrine of plenary inspiration. Infallible biblical witnesses are based on doctrines describing the virgin birth of Christ and the saving power of Christ's death. In addition, are other doctrines describing His physical resurrection from the tomb and His return to glory at the last day.

We must go on to question the adequacy of the image. The image blurs a fundamental distinction. That distinction is between WHAT God does and statements ABOUT what God does. To believe in the substitutionary doctrine of the atonement may be very different from believing that Jesus Christ died for me.

Believing the doctrine almost inevitably becomes a substitute for committing one's life to the God whom the doctrine is trying to describe. Then, the following statement emerges. "Can any doctrinal statement that is formed of the human intellect truly define divinity that is set apart from the totality of human understanding?" Doctrinal statements are not in themselves the truth. God does not give us doctrines. He gives Himself in Jesus Christ and the doctrines are no more than our way of attempting to think through what that gift means. We must, to be sure, think it through as well as we possibly can, so what we think must not become the object of our faith.

The right of private judgment does not mean that I can make up my own gospel. It simply means that I must make my own decision about the gospel that is proclaimed to me. No one else can make my own decision about the gospel that is proclaimed to me. No one else can make that decision but me. The right of private judgment also means the need for a personal decision. In these terms, there are few matters that could be more characteristic of the spirit of Protestantism.

Part of the urgency of the Protestant message has always been the insistence that I must decide for or against something. We must decide about something that comes to us, rather than about something that comes from us.

Truth can therefore be found in the following false images. First, Protestantism is primarily affirmative and is negative only in the sense that not to affirm anything is to deny something else. Second, Protestantism is an interpretation of the wholeness of the Christian faith rather than a diluted form of it. Third,

Protestian has a genuine content that can be described. However, the descriptive statement must always point beyond themselves and must never become the object of faith. Fourth, Protestantism is man's creation of a faith of his own. Protestantism exists to serve that gospel. It is the good news that in Jesus Christ, God was reconciling the world unto Himself.

The Catholicity of Protestantism plunges into the sixteenth century movement known as the reformation or religious revolt against the church. The closest assessment of the Reformation was their central concern to give the biblical faith a chance for a real hearing. They felt it had been stifled and distorted by the church for many centuries. Far from revolting against the church, they were trying to reform it. The Reformers tried to call attention to the faith that had brought it into being many centuries before.

The Protestant Reformation was a deeper plunge into the meaning of the gospel. The Reformers felt that loyalty must be given to that gospel. The subject and object of that loyalty was Jesus Christ. They felt that their fidelity to the church must be measured by the degree of the church's fidelity to the gospel. Protestantism asserts that a collection of writings composed between 750 B.C. and A.D. 150 should be the source and standard of the church's life until the end of time. It is known as the Scriptures.

Protestants believe that the Scriptures are not Christ, but it houses Christ. Jesus Christ is found within it. The purpose of the Scripture is simply to witness Jesus Christ. Jesus Christ is the King of Kings and the Lord of Lords of mankind and the Scriptures. The whole point of the Holy Bible (Scriptures) is that it should imply Jesus Christ. This, then, illustrates the authority of the Scripture in the life of the church.

Concern for the Holy Spirit also lies behind the tension between Scripture and tradition. The question that now concerns us is, by what means does the Spirit of Christ do his work in the church? The conventional Protestant answer has been that the Scripture is the channel through which the power of the Holy Spirit flows. Protestantism believes that Roman Catholicism has permitted so many tributaries marked tradition to enter the channel. As a result, the original springs of living water have become impure and marred.

Protestant concerns point up to two issues that divide Protestantism and Roman Catholicism. First, what Protestants fear about "catholic power" and second, the problem of authority. The following example provides a general overview.

It is recognized in Catholicism that something has gone wrong in the relationship between God and man. In most cultures, an intermediary is necessary to make situations right again. Such an intermediary is a priest. A priest is God's representative to man. He has authority to communicate and interpret God's purpose to the people. The priest is also man's representative to God. He, the priest, intercedes for the people. The priest offers sacrifices to the deity in the hope of placating Him and getting His forgiveness for sins. Therefore, the calling of the Christian man is to lead a life worthy of the calling to which he has been called. The calling refers to the lifestyle that must characterize a Christian, the priest, in all that he does as a Christian. This includes loving God with the mind and worshipping God in the unity of the Word and sacraments.

Because Protestants are loyal, they are critical. Because Jesus Christ is the same yesterday, today and forever, there must be new attempts to see what Christ means today. Tensions and conflicts within Protestantism and Catholicism will not disappear. Some of the particular tensions and conflicts may fade away. However, new tensions and conflicts will divide the ranks and questions yet unasked will be the occasion of future controversies.

In conclusion, theologians will not produce a synthesis and even if they could, a synthesis will never meet our deepest need. These theologians can point us to one who is greater than all syntheses. In their descriptions, we having some insight can become more aware for ourselves and share in turn what we have seen.

## John Wesley

John Wesley is the father of Methodism and a product of Protestantism. Mr. Wesley came to Georgia, in 1735, to begin his movement and beliefs on how the church should be patterned. People in this movement were called Methodists because of the evangelistic teachings and work of John Wesley, Charles Wesley, George Whitfield and others in the first half of the 18th century. Their teachings were derived from the methodical study and worship (adhering to a method) practiced by the founders in their "Holy Club" at Oxford University in 1729.

After returning to Europe, Wesley later sent Dr. Thomas Coke, an Anglican priest, to establish the Methodist's church government. Dr. Coke was to push for the acceptance of Methodism by all as the real form of worship. Dr. Coke called a conference on December 25, 1784, in Baltimore, Maryland, to formally organize the Methodist denomination.

Wesley's chief contribution to history was to build a people for God. His conviction was that he believed in the people called Methodists. Wesley believed God had raised up Methodists as a distinctive witness.

John Wesley identified the Methodist people as those who were to be a sanctuary for sinners desiring to flee from the wrath to come. Methodists were loving members of a New Testament fellowship that came to life in the eighteenth century. They were those distinguished not by particular opinions or modes of worship, but, by their confidence in God's grace to meet fully every need. Methodists were also those people who were to spread scriptural holiness throughout the land. They were not a revision of christianity but its renewal.

Wesley counselled his successors to remain steadfast to Jesus Christ and Methodism. He stated that he was not concerned whether Methodist people would ever cease to exist either in Europe or America. Instead, Wesley was concerned that the Methodists would only exist as a dead sect. He was also concerned that Methodist people would have the form of religion without the power of God. Wesley felt that this would undoubtedly be the case unless they held fast to the doctrine, spirit and discipline of Methodism. Methodist people must hold fast to the church structure for which Methodism was first set.

Wesley believed that a Methodist faithful to its heritage could endure permanently with Protestant christianity. He thus labored unsparingly to fix the Methodists upon such a foundation as was likely to show forth their faith by works. Otherwise, Wesley thought that God would root out the memorial of them from the earth. Wesley instituted programs to focus on the care for the needy, the sick and underprivileged. These programs served as an outreach that would be an extension of one's relationship with Jesus Christ. Wesley strongly emphasized ignoring ceremonial rituals for establishing or maintaining a relationship with God.

Blacks became acquainted with church formalities and structures through the Methodist Church. Introduction to church structure and formalities came when Harry Hoosier and Richard Allen attended the first Methodist conference in Baltimore, Maryland as observers. While attending the conference, Hoosier and Allen were not permitted to serve as delegates, voters or as ministerial participants. They were not permitted to serve as delegates, voters or ministerial participants because they were Black.

After the Methodist conference in Baltimore, Richard Allen became the founder of the first organized Black church in America. In 1800, the Methodist Church was the first denomination, in America, to ordain Blacks as preachers.

# CHAPTER 6
## *WHAT IS THE BLACK CHURCH?*

The Black church's introduction into American history came in the late 1700's. The thrust to develop Black America's church came as a result of the need to relieve Black people from oppression. The church served to educate, spiritually cultivate and permit cultural freedom of expression. The church also served to provide a refuge from social injustices and abuses. It was also perceived as the central place within the black community where major, significant and noteworthy events took place. In other words, the church was the center and primary focal point in the community.

Historically, the Black church has always evolved and emerged during a period of severe poverty, depression and disadvantagement. For example, in pre-Civil War days, the African Methodist Episcopal Church (Black America's oldest denomination) got its beginning. While the Great Depression in the

1930's was devastating humanity, holiness, apostolic and pentecostal churches flourished.

The church's primary objective during these particular phases in history was to assist the less fortunate in every possible way. This meant giving hope to its oppressed citizens by indoctrinating them with a sense of self-worth. Encouragement and propelling them successfully as disciples into societal affairs were other objectives of the Black church. The Black church lacked knowledge and information about how to construct an institution of excellence. Therefore, it was necessary for them to use a prototype all ready in existence.

For identity, psychological satisfaction and spiritual fulfillment, the Black church incubated the Protestant Church government structure. The Black church, however, birthed an organization religiously different to fit its culture and purposes. This is certainly not to say that the black church is any less religious than its counterpart.

On the contrary, the black religious experience has been seen as having a type of "religiosity" that our counterparts have been slow to move into. It can safely be said that the authenticity of the black religious experience can only be captured within the realm of the black church.

A majority of the Black churches are an offspring of Protestantism. Black Americans warmly embraced membership into Protestant churches. However, Black Americans always forced themselves to become independent entities by developing their own churches. The reason was simply a feeling of uncomfortableness and an insatiable desire to rule their own. With this philosophy in mind, it became imperative for the Black church to achieve social and economic freedom.

Previous experiences under oppressive dictatorship unconsciously relayed messages to Black leaders on what to expect, when one possessed keys to unlimited social and economic possibilities. The Black church was then used as the most viable means of achieving and acquiring freedom. As a result, Black leaders began building their churches to take Blacks far beyond the imprisonment of slave mentality. They wanted to create specific services to suffice the spiritual, mental, social and economic freedom needs of Blacks.

What is essentially the Black church? The Black church is a religious entity that is *traditionally* led by a Black pastor with a predominantly Black congregation. The structure and organization of the Black church is Protestant in nature. However, it is designed to influence the local community with social services for the needy, underprivileged and for the betterment of their brethren. Spiritual efforts include indoctrinating its citizens with biblical principles, morals and ethics that develop character. The primary service of the Black church is to teach and instruct Blacks on how to be dependent on God as their real source.

Most are aware of the movement within the Methodist church to do cross-cultural appointments. There are several in place around the country. However, this is more the exception than the norm. This does change the paradigm of the black church.

# CHAPTER 7
## *THE MISSION OF THE BLACK CHURCH*

When the message of freedom was not penetrating the hearts of White slave owners, helping underprivileged Blacks became a primary focus of the Black church. In the minds of many Black church leaders and parishioners, crusading for equality was a champion cause. The mission of the Black church has always been focussed on meeting the spiritual, social and educational needs of Black people.

Black people always needed a place of refuge during slavery times to express their dissatisfactions and to air out frustrations. They sought to maintain a form of identity and bond with others in like conditions. Blacks felt it was necessary to devise tactics to form a social network to persuade political changes. The church was this place of refuge and it inadvertently adopted social welfare as its real mission.

The foundation and mission for the Black church, as established by our Black forefathers, has never been challenged. The real mission of the church has become faulty. It does not support what God had originally left as a blueprint for the church's mission. The true mission of the Black church must now be reevaluated.

## Right Motives - Wrong Direction

The church has a product everybody needs, with a world market and really no competition. The gospel of Jesus Christ is indispensable to the eternal welfare of all men and no other institution has this message, this mandate or this market. A business man would make a killing -- but what of the church? The church is no longer unique, but dysfunctional. She is now positioned to compete with community organizations working for the improvement of society.

Black churches have neglected their unique mission and task of propagating the gospel. It has defected to giving social, political and economic affairs priority.

The church has defaulted and the whole world feels the impact. We should feel confident that service clubs, lodges, and community organizations are not going to proclaim the gospel of Jesus Christ, nor support the church's mission. Proper focus for the mission of the church usually is hindered, not through the laziness of Christians, but through the busyness of Christians in the wrong directions.

Ministers, for the most part, are hard-pressed, overworked and underpaid, with sometimes not very much to show for all of their labors. The leaders have failed at this very point. They do not have any inner resource. Some ministers have no direction in which to help unleash the motivation that is within the members of their congregations.

Religious leaders are constantly placed in the forefront of society to verbalize the people's requirements for satisfactory solutions to their concerns. Oftentimes it is to policymakers. Meeting the needs of the people is important. However, the order for the mission of the church has been reversed and it is proving to be ineffective.

## Evangelism

The primary mission for the church is evangelism. The chief end of evangelism is that men should hear, really hear the good news that God's kingdom is a live option for them. That evangelism affects their own here and now. That God's answer is a Person. God's gift was a Person. God's gift was His Son. God's total answer to man's total need is Jesus Christ. No one has ever tried Jesus Christ whatever his need and found Him inadequate. Never has a man related personally to Jesus Christ and been disappointed.

Our world is starving for people who have found something worth believing. It wants people who are prepared to declare and commend the gospel that speaks of THE WAY to a lost generation.

The world we live in craves for THE TRUTH from those who have not been brainwashed into believing there is no hope. The world needs the gospel that gives THE LIFE to those whose prevailing philosophy is one of despair and death.

The business of the disciple is called to present Jesus Christ in the power of the Holy Spirit. The disciple is called to present Jesus Christ in love, humility and sincerity. They are to show what Jesus claimed to be, the revealer of God and Savior of the world.

Evangelism is not selling but telling a message and demonstrating the power of God; reporting good news. It is speaking and acting with the authority of Jesus Christ in the power and love, the Holy Spirit. Evangelism does not resort to canned speeches or sales gimmicks for its effectiveness; nor does it rely on Madison Avenue pitches.

Effective evangelism is not zeal, passion or rhetorical overkill. Rightly understood, it is not the work of a person at all. It is the work of the Holy Spirit. The Holy Spirit entered history for this purpose. He indwelt the Church at Pentecost to do His evangelistic work through her. The Holy Spirit will perform His evangelistic task through any man who will yield to His infilling and submit to His control.

This does not mean that legitimate methods are to be abandoned nor that the disciple can ignore training and study and personal application. It does mean that He does not depend upon any of these in and of themselves for effectiveness. It does mean He wants the best of methods and discipline and application made servant of the Holy Spirit.

Nominal christianity and leadership simply has not got what it takes. It is one big reason for the failure of the church to be a purifying, redeeming force in North American's social structure. Nominal christianity is nothing more than the veneer of christian custom and culture passed down generation-by-generation in increasingly ineffective doses. Getting farther and farther from the source of its original power, it deteriorates, becomes progressively thinner, more innocuous. It is the handing down of the fruits of faith without the root. Nominal christianity is the form without the substance and the shadow without the reality. It holds no real promise of transforming men, women and youth into a vital relationship with Jesus Christ.

It is the supreme plan of God to channel His divine resources through His church to the world. The Church is God's divine agent to distribute His message of love, health, healing, salvation and eternal security.

The diagram, in the figure on the following page, represents current church conditions and shows that divine resources are not reaching its intended destination -- the world. As shown, the problem is found in the distribution channel -- the church.

Why is there this gross failure of the church to get on with its primary and urgent task of evangelism? Crucial lessons to grasp in evangelism are that we are engaged in spiritual warfare. Yet, we are not left powerless in overcoming

## FIGURE 9
### THE SPIRITUAL LAW OF GOD'S DIVINE ECONOMY

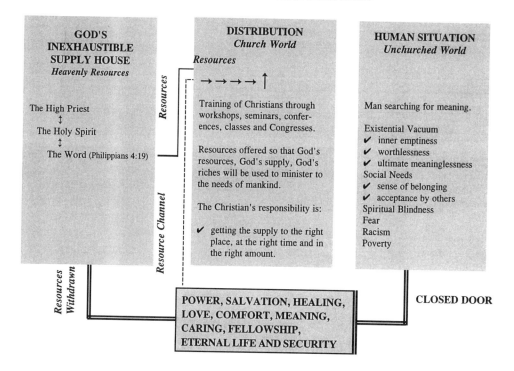

**GOD'S INEXHAUSTIBLE SUPPLY HOUSE**
*Heavenly Resources*

The High Priest
↕
The Holy Spirit
↕
The Word (Philippians 4:19)

*Resources*

*Resource Channel*

*Resources Withdrawn*

**DISTRIBUTION**
*Church World*

*Resources*

→ → → → ↑

Training of Christians through workshops, seminars, conferences, classes and Congresses.

Resources offered so that God's resources, God's supply, God's riches will be used to minister to the needs of mankind.

The Christian's responsibility is:

✔ getting the supply to the right place, at the right time and in the right amount.

**HUMAN SITUATION**
*Unchurched World*

Man searching for meaning.

Existential Vacuum
✔ inner emptiness
✔ worthlessness
✔ ultimate meaninglessness
Social Needs
✔ sense of belonging
✔ acceptance by others
Spiritual Blindness
Fear
Racism
Poverty

**POWER, SALVATION, HEALING, LOVE, COMFORT, MEANING, CARING, FELLOWSHIP, ETERNAL LIFE AND SECURITY**

**CLOSED DOOR**

adversity. The main weapons that Paul discovered that had *"divine power to destroy strongholds"* were the weapons of *"the sword of the Spirit,"* which is *the Word of God* and *prayer*.

Without some understanding of the will and plan of God, so much of our work can be little more than "beating the air." Knowing God's will and obeying it is worth infinitely more than endlessly toiling away in our own strength. It is the desire and purpose of the Holy Spirit to make known to us the will of God. The Holy Spirit then gives us the strength and power to do it.

If Christians lack the desire to evangelize, then our conferences, crusades, strategies and schemes are all in vain. God-called leaders must use disciples to take the message of divine forgiveness. They must preach the assurance of the presence of the risen Lord and supernatural grace to the unchurched world.

## Disciples

The leader's primary responsibility is to hear from God and to put into legislation, the "mind of God." The "mind of God" will always meet the needs of the people. The needs of the people will never fall in meeting the purpose of God. God created the universe and man and He is capable of ordering and controlling its existence.

Jesus gathered twelve of his closest followers around Him and gave them words of wisdom concerning the founding of this band. He ordained twelve that they should be with Him and that He might send them forth to preach. Its function is clear: to be with him, to be closely united with Him and to go out to tell the good news.

The mission of the Black church is to train and equip disciples with purpose and vision. By doing so, disciples will inevitably carry out the vision of the leader. This will help meet the needs of the congregation and the community.

Disciples are followers and an extension of the leader. Their purpose is essential in developing the leader's vision. Disciples are to maintain proper focus and function of Christ's mission for the church. The more disciples are trained and equipped to fulfill the mission of the church, the more successful the church becomes. In addition, the leader is less likely to become personally involved in community or social affairs. Instead, the leader will constantly be in communion with God to meet the spiritual needs of the people. Spiritual not civil.

Moses is an example of one having an intimate relationship with God to lead people. God gave him the Ten Commandments. To help him carry out those commandments, Jethro, his father-in-law, told him to ordain elders. The elders would help Moses carry out the mind of God. Disciples were the answer to this problem.

Where there is no leadership, there is chaos. When there is no voice to speak and provide direction, there is also chaos. Where there is leadership with distorted ideologies and theologies, there is a confused people. The leader with the vision is the church. Without a vision, the people will perish. It is critical that the leader impart God's vision, focus and purpose to the people. Why? The leader is an oracle of God to the people in relaying His mind.

Isaiah 54 states that our ways are not God's ways and our thoughts are not His thoughts. In every case as we pattern ourselves after Christ, we are to envision His purpose, ways and thoughts. We, as Christians, are to live above circumstances that inhibit, restrict and confine. Discipleship restores order and properly systematizes God's purpose for mankind and his success.

## Disciples As Evangelists

The great commission is binding on every Christian. The imperatives are: Go! (Mark 16:15); Witness! (Acts 1:8); and, Love! (John 13).

It was never the intention of our Lord that the work of the ministry be left to the professionals or a few "full-time workers." Every disciple was to have a place in the program of propagating the world with the Gospel. Rightly understood, the Church of Jesus Christ is a lay movement. The work of the ministry belongs to the person in the pew.

Persecution in Jerusalem scattered the Church and everywhere they were scattered they witnessed. God used persecution to sow laymen everywhere and they witnessed everywhere. Actually, this is the only way the world can be reached -- every disciple is to be an evangelist in the world where he lives, or works and socializes. He is there. How can he expect someone who is not there to evangelize his world?

The witness of the New Testament disciple was not a sales pitch. They simply shared what they had received each in his own way. Theirs was not a formally prepared, carefully worked-out presentation with a gimmick to manipulate conversation and for an on-the-spot decision.

Witnesses of the New Testament disciple was the spontaneous, irrepressible, effervescent enthusiasm of men who had met the most fascinating person who ever lived. They had had an encounter with Jesus Christ and it simply could not be concealed. Their "school of witnessing" was the school of the Holy Ghost in which they matriculated continuously. The witnesses were not indoctrinated, they were oriented. They witnessed, not because they had to, but because they could not help it.

Church leaders agree that the answer to the church's problem is to be found in motivation. What is motivation? Motivation is the process of arousing, sustaining and regulating action. The task of the **leader**, after training the people in discipleship, will not be so much in motivating others, but helping to harness the motivation that is already there.

What is the mission of the church? The intimate relationship of a leader with God, who is to voice God's purpose, impart vision and train the people to become disciples and evangelists. Their duties are to carry out God's original design for mankind -- they are to rule, reign, subdue and multiply.

# CHAPTER 8
## *CHRISTIANITY FOR BLACKS IN AMERICA*

### Freedom Defined

The foundation and basis for America's religious fundamentals, doctrine, theology and guide for living, are all taken from the Holy Bible -- the real source of liberation. For centuries, the Bible has been recognized as the Holy Scriptures. It has molded the life, cultures and thoughts of Christianity. We hear in it not the words of men but the Word of God.

The Holy Scriptures are a writing or a collection of writings on which God has laid His hand. By God's Word, we mean the Word which God Himself speaks and speaks to men. In His Word, God does not simply impart truth about Himself, but rather He opens His heart to mankind. The Word of God is the self-disclosure of God. He opens his mind to man and is the heart of the book and the criterion by which **ALL** must be measured. From Genesis to Revelation, the Holy Bible states that God came to show forth Himself and to liberate those that were held in captivity.

If the Holy Bible is the real source of liberation, questions posed by many Blacks to be answered include the following. What God does the white man really serve? What religion does the white man serve? If they serve Yahweh or Elohim, then who's in error, God or the white man? Is the God of freedom a colorless God? Is the God of freedom a just God who vindicates wrong? Or, does God sanction captivity and there is indeed no freedom? If the latter is true, then can the Holy Bible still be seen as a service of liberation? If so, to what extent?

Luke 4:18-19 sheds light on the answer. It tells of God's Son who came to show the essence of His Father to all mankind and to all people.

> *The Spirit of the Lord (my Father) is upon me, because he hath anointed me to preach the gospel to the poor; He hath sent me to heal the broken-hearted, to preach deliverance to the captives, and recovering of sight to the blind, to set at liberty them that are bruised, To preach the acceptable year of the Lord.*

68

Other illuminators presented in the Holy Bible, before and preceding Luke 4 are Isaiah 61 and Luke 19. Both are identical and reiterate freedom.

To understand mankind, one must first look at God. Looking at God determines what mankind's purpose is. It also helps mankind to visualize God's design for him. To understand God's purpose and design is to know God and **freedom**.

Jesus Christ, clothed in His Father's authority, was sent to officiate on our behalf. He was to empower us with the same authority given by His Father. As a joint heir with Jesus Christ and His Father (God), mankind is considered equal in all respects of kinship. This includes the spiritual and soulish makeup of his being. The essence of Jesus Christ's mission was to proclaim liberty and to eradicate the effects of slavery on all levels. This embraces not only physical slavery, but it is inclusive of emotional and mental slavery as well. Slavery can then be seen as that which causes bondage in every way.

The Scriptures proclaimed in the New Covenant indicate that God brought together two different races of people. They were the Jews and the Gentiles. In His rebuke to the discriminators, Jesus made it plain that no one kind of being had any more superiority than the other in any way, shape or form. He called the discriminators, hypocrites.

Christianity and religion in America for the Black man has meant limitless struggles to obtain biblical freedom. Biblical freedom is the means of worshiping God with all races of people and cultures. Biblical freedom is also the verbal and written expression, on all issues, that confront mankind in America. Biblical freedom, for all, with liberality.

## Religious Racism -- Fear vs. Love

The greatest underlying cause behind religious racial tension, division, slavery and unconscious mental bondage in America is **fear**. It was fear that caused the unity in worship between Blacks and whites to halt in the early 1900's. It was fear that caused a split in the Azusa Street's Black and white worship arena. That fear has formed two of the largest denominations in America. They are the Church of God in Christ and the Assembly of God. One is Black and the other is white.

It was fear that overwhelmed the American mentality. It continued to twist that mentality and used it to undermine the Black man's freedom. Fear even destroyed Black and white unity in worship and hindered Black and white cohesiveness under God. It is fear that continues to separate us. It separates us in three major areas. First, it separates us on the basis of our understanding of God. Second, it separates us on the basis of God's action in the world with humanity. Third, it separates us on our understanding of how we perceive that action as agents of God.

The answer to the problem of fear is love. Fear is never a product of love. Fear destroys while love builds. Love must always be first and foremost in the minds of the people. Love must be exercised so freedom prevails and fear is dispelled. Love knows no color nor does it superimpose itself over one's mentality to cause division and strife. Love always stimulates and provokes the positive. Simultaneously, it depolarizes the negative and makes it less prominent.

Love is the only way to grasp another human being in the innermost core of his personality. No one can become fully aware of the very essence of another human being unless he loves him.

## Purpose

Whites were chosen by God to bring Blacks out of idol worship. They were to provide Blacks with necessary resources essential to their well-being during the transition from apostasy to monotheism. Contrary to Black popular opinion, the white man is not the devil nor a cell from him. Over time, satanic forces have distorted the purpose of the white person by infiltrating many of their souls with an attitude of prejudice and arrogance.

Misplaced love has instilled a division between the races. It has caused each race of people to close themselves within the confines of their own culture. This helps each race to become desensitized to all other cultures and cultural experiences. Therefore, we devalue others and their worth inside the mainstream of humanity. Specifically, the many races of people have become oblivious to all others.

These actions have strengthened communication gaps, inverted conscious awareness and stimulated racial division. Thus, satanic forces have made us (both whites and Blacks) out to be irrational imbeciles. Under any other circumstances, Blacks and whites would behave intelligently given an awareness and a clear definition of the real problem.

John Newton is the writer of the Amazing Grace hymn. However, it stands reasonable to believe that John Newton did not know his real purpose. If he did, Newton would not have made money (exploit) from the sale of African slaves to white Americans. It also stands reasonable to believe that those who contributed to the Dred Scott Supreme Court decision never knew their purpose. If they did, they would never have stated that the Black man was less than a man, while the Holy Bible and a prayer opened the Court for business. What has caused the dwarfed mentality and loss of focus on the sole purpose and reality of the white man to Blacks in America? Frankly, the lack of understanding of purpose.

## The Black Preacher

The Black preacher is the freest person in Black America. Why is he considered to be so free? He is always perceived to be free because he does not have to answer directly to any "outside" authority. The Black preacher is also considered free because his primary and only responsibility are to provide answers to his people on their plight as American citizens. The Black preacher's position of freedom usually becomes endangered when he partakes in institutionalism. His freedom also becomes endangered when he partakes in religious educational stratums that override his focus.

Institutionalism and religious educational stratums are psychological and societal weapons that dulls the perception to the real issues. The real issues are the Black man's purpose, call and commitment to God. Educational stratums have been unfruitful logistical systems of order. The following are some of the reasons they are unfruitful.

The first unfruitful system are religious educational stratums or what is better known as theological seminaries. This particular system is responsible for clothing and poisoning the liberated spiritual thinking of Black preachers with polished beliefs and values that are absurd.

Many have doctrinized the Holy Bible to fit polluted thinking about God and his mandates. For example, seminaries have provided doctrines about the Holy Spirit that says "every saved person has the Holy Spirit of God, so you do not need to speak in tongues." They have also taught the idiotic notion that God heals and blesses some people. Black preachers have also been doctrinized with other statements that state some Christians have to suffer with sickness and poverty for Jesus Christ's sake. These are nothing more than religious lies. Their training is exemplified and "passed on" through their Church.

There are even theological seminaries that make their students sign statements that they will not "speak with other tongues" before admittance is final for student tenure. These procedures and doctrines are strategies to be carried back into the community to maintain a slave mentality, instead of God-freedom consciousness.

Second, institutions and religious educational stratums have a tendency to force many Black preachers to ignore and abandon what the Black man's purpose in christianity is. They also force them to ignore what each Black person's purpose is to God, his society and the world. Instead, the focus returns to seminary doctrines that are humanized and to an institution that purports individualism. Third, institutions and religious educational stratums are the reason for many spiritual moves of God being turned into civil rights movements.

Theological seminaries are essential to the growth of any spiritual leader. Through strong curriculums, students can benefit and be challenged intellectually to broadened their horizons through biblical studies. Structured environments in seminaries provide students with a sound foundation and a path on which to grow. Bible scholars, who are seminary instructors, provide us with valuable insight into the past, present and future of biblical events.

As we propel into the future, participants in current biblical events can record happenings to provide a legacy to future generations. The structure of seminaries is to accurately portray these events, while providing a basis to plan and train new students. Seminaries are the custodians of history, the teachers of principles and the foundation for study and research.

Nothing is more detrimental to the growth of any race of people than an "unlearned" leader. Knowledge gained through seminary training eliminates a potential tragedy. It takes more than shouting and verbally espousing your adoration and praise of God. It takes study and training under a "learned" professional. Such can be found through seminaries. Your relationship with God and the Holy Spirit, with the guidance of a learned educator, provides balance.

Sales of biblical material strongly indicate the quest for knowledge of the supernatural. How can we progress spiritually without the educational foundation for which we are to believe and spiritually grow? It is my belief that seminaries offer the training and knowledge vital to the growth of any student of the gospel of Jesus Christ.

Spiritual issues must be addressed by Black preachers who have been educated by God and through seminary training. Spiritual issues are to come from God-ordained institutions and those who are in a position of influence. They must take the lead as role models to remove the burden placed on the Black community to make changes. Authentic role models are required when a community has no vision. Role models are also needed when the community has not reached a level of understanding that quantifies respect. If not, the Black preacher's freedom then as Black America's real "free" person becomes a boomerang of previous stances. That is, continued frustration in getting biblical freedom will prevail.

## Civil Rights

Many Black preachers have managed to turn every move of God toward freedom into civil rights movements. Though civil rights movements have made unprecedented strides in obtaining equality for all mankind, the issue of a divine move of God about christianity in America has been misinterpreted. Somehow, spiritual issues have been turned into civil rights issues. Spiritual does affect the social, but should be qualified appropriately.

On the flip side of this issue is the need for Black leaders, particularly preachers, to go beyond social and political welfare. They should deal with the spiritual plight of the Black man. Once Black preachers address where Christ fits within the confines of this issue, the answer to the Black man's liberation from slavery could very well be answered.

Civil rights issues have become more important than spiritual issues. The discussion following provides why it began to replace God-christianity in America with rights-christianity in America.

The prevalent erroneous misconception that some white people have is that once the Black man received freedom, they would always need to depend on him for survival. Nothing could be further from the truth. Black people are intelligent beings. They are capable of ruling with excellence in any situation they are confronted with, without dependency.

Century after century, records indicate that Blacks have made outstanding universal achievements. These achievements have left and continue to leave indelible impacts. It is recorded in history that Blacks are responsible for designing and building Ethiopian and Egyptian pyramids. They invented paper, were the originator of architecture and constructed sailing boats. Blacks are recorded as having started the domestication of animals. Also recorded are the development of maps, clocks, calendars, the pipe organ and glass. Regardless of these phenomenal accomplishments, whites have relayed and felt as though they were the only ones who had all the answers.

Whites have viewed themselves as the caretaker of the good. Whites felt they should help the less fortunate by keeping the good dependent on spoon-feeding. As a result, slavery continues to ride on. Once again, to recapitulate an earlier premise, the primary purpose for whites was to evangelize Blacks and provide resources for independent growth.

Over the years, Blacks have used riotous behavior to get the attention of those in control to view the real issue. That is, evangelize us and give us freedom in all areas. However, revolts by Blacks are perceived by whites as no solution to the problem. Many whites feel this is a threat to confuse the issue of who's really in control.

Social systems developed by whites say for Blacks to join in with what we're doing. The inference is that they can show you how to win. This has been highly misleading. Social systems are and have been nothing more than perplexing mazes that give very little answers. These systems are controlling mechanisms that are designed to keep the white man informed and abreast of changes within the Black community. Specifically, it informs them on behavioral thinking patterns and spontaneous reactions of Black people.

The social system conformity ideology states the "don't challenge the system" process. It attempts to force you to understand it and to fight within it so you can win against it. This method of winning still perpetrates slavery to win freedom. Many times it has either been futile or too late.

The Black church then became involved with the rights of its people. The church rode these issues to intervene and provide refuge. The church sought to provide answers to the "why we do what we do, and why we'll keep on doing what we've done until freedom comes." Thus, civil rights christianity.

This point must be reiterated. Blacks are not interested in reliving slavery times. They are concerned with moving forward in time. Blacks want the best that can be offered socially, financially and educationally. Blacks are solely interested in the same freedom, equal rights and opportunities available to all citizens in this country. According to the Emancipation Proclamation, it's *free to all*.

## The Power of the Black Church in Politics

Although civil rights issues are now in the forefront of the political agenda, politicians have disrespected and ignored the power of the Black church in America. The work of civil rights leaders such as Dr. Martin Luther King, Ralph Abernathy and Jesse Jackson, through the Black church, has opened and pulled-up the veil off from politicians. These leaders have made politicians aware of the real power the Black church and its community possesses.

From this unveiling, politicians are now beginning to realize that the way of reaching mass numbers of Blacks is through the church. Regardless of whether it has been more civil than spiritual, the church does have power and politicians are well aware of this. Politicians and other recognized authority figures further realize that Black churches and their leaders can no longer be ignored. They know that the Black church possesses the ability to sway people's opinions and this influence eventually effects those in positions of power. In many black churches, it has become a common place before elections to see politicians show up at a prime time church service. This is done to introduce themselves and to inject a "sound bite." Afterwards, many promptly leave that church to try to secure yet another "sound bite" opportunity.

Politicians and elected officials are confident now more than ever, that Black church leaders are positioned in the heart of America. When Black leaders use their power effectively, these leaders can dictate who sits in rule over their interests. On the spiritual side, the Black church is taking the position of getting more involved with politics. This is not to just protect their interests, but to tear down the walls of the "Church vs. State" doctrine. The church, previously defined and discussed, is the real group of legislators.

## The Final Solution

The first solution to Black America's christianity dilemma is to understand one's purpose. The next step is to be in line with that purpose. The third step is to trust the God who designed the purpose and proper order for the universe and mankind. These solutions are crucial for the Black race, as they prepare to go into the 21st century.

What has christianity in America been for Black people? It has been confusion on the issue of the suppression of biblical freedom. Christianity has been confusion of the white man's purpose, but hope for freedom. In addition, it has been a thrust for freedom without restraints, in becoming equal in all respects and on all levels.

# CHAPTER 9
## *THE QUALIFICATIONS OF A LEADER TO DISCIPLE OTHERS*

It is not enough to be born again. We must have a relationship with Jesus Christ and an uncompromised Christian experience.

A leader is defined as one called by God to guide and rule over those assigned to his domain. He acts and serves as an overseer. He leads people through adverse situations by imparting vision. A leader serves as a captain to steer a ship through life's narrow passageways.

A leader's specific purpose is defined by God. God gives the leader His mind to affect the world. The vision given the leader is in part and requires his total dependence upon God for substance, direction and success. This vision, thus, becomes his purpose for a season.

When a leader approaches his vision in faith, he may be somewhat apprehensive. However, his spirit man is charged with such power and confidence, that he usually forges forward with anticipated expectancy. His encounter with God has so impressed him that he cannot help satisfy this omnipotent being with nothing more than obedience.

When he returns from the spiritual realm to the natural to begin working out his "own soul's salvation," the leader must seek godly counsel. Godly counsel will help him interpret the vision and receive direction to fulfill his call and purpose. The leader must be sure that he without fault, relays God's mind as was received. When this is done, the people's perception will be in line with his delivery.

The primary area that determines the leader's effectiveness is found in his ability to hear God and to deliver God's message. Seeking counsel and obeying God's direction on where to seek godly counsel is important. This will determine how accurate the interpretation of God's mind and will is to those assigned to his domain. His domain, in turn, affects all others. Godly counsellors are a key to successful leadership. Godly counsellors will always first instruct leaders to know the purpose of his ministry and to prepare accordingly.

Second, the leader is counselled to get the proper spiritual and educational training. A good leader is trained to think and study. Third, he is taught that every leader called by God *must* be equipped to lead in the areas of stewardship, evangelism, education and worship. Fourth, godly counsellors direct the leader to prepare to have his God-given vision challenged for its authenticity.

## Qualities Of A Good Leader

The most thrilling chapters in God's call to leadership begins in Genesis 17:1. God called Abraham and said unto him: *"I AM the Almighty God; walk before Me and be thou perfect."* In this wonderful title, God reveals to Abraham His power and His all sufficiency.

God reveals His power to protect and preserve man through all the vicissitudes, troubles, sorrows and problems of life. In addition, God shows His leadership ability as the true Shepherd who cares for His sheep. God also reveals to Abraham His power to supply every spiritual and physical need.

There is no need of any kind, in any human life, that cannot be met fully by the Eternal God who wears the name "Almighty." This is illustrated in the 18th chapter of Genesis. Here, Sarah and Abraham were struggling to believe that Sarah would bear a child in her old age. In that instance, God asked the penetrating question that paralyzed her to fear: "Is any thing too hard for the Lord?"

Second, God called and commanded Abraham to *"walk before Me."* In talking with Abraham, God shows him the manner of life and the path to be pursued through life. God assured him if he would walk with Him, He would make him strong, vigorous and active. God also showed Abraham that he would be a conqueror and the father of many nations. This reveals the true success and blessed results which comes to a leader who will follow a godly walk and stays in fellowship with the Lord. It confirms that if a leader has a constant abiding in the Holy Spirit and a constant feeding on the Word of God blessed results follow. This lifestyle is always fruitful which brings glory to God and blessings to others.

Finally, He commanded Abraham to *"be thou perfect."* The Greek interpretation of the word perfect is rendered being perfect in one's attitude toward God, to trust, and not be focussed on one's sinlessness.

There are many references in the Word of God of His ultimate purpose for His people. God does not want His leader to be occupied with the dead things of this world, but with the living things of heaven. For the things that are highly esteemed by men are an abomination in the sight of God. The pleasures of this world are dead in the sight of God and have no spiritual value in the leader's life. God considers it sin.

When God commanded Abraham to be perfect, He was not implying that he would be sinless. God was calling for a perfect attitude and conduct toward Him. He was also calling for him to resist temptation and to turn a deaf ear to the callings of the world. God wanted Abraham to take a positive stand against sin and the attractions which satan offers.

The unfolding of God's revelation to meet the human needs and solve man's dilemma through His called-leader continues in the book of Exodus. All of heaven's attention is focussed around the scene of communication which God made to Moses at the burning bush. God spoke to Moses and said unto him, *"I AM the Lord: and I appeared unto Abraham, Issac and unto Jacob, by the name of GOD ALMIGHTY, but My name Jehovah was not known to them."*

God first appeared unto Abraham and identified himself as *"I AM the Almighty God. "* His purpose for calling him is revealed in their conversation. God being a God of faith, looks for the man who will believe, trust, obey and fulfill that faith imparted to him regardless of circumstances.

God called Abraham out of ignorance and oddity to preserve a godly lineage through whom all the nations of the earth would be blessed. Abraham's assignment was to demonstrate what faith could do. His assignment was to prove to the world that there is a true and living God who wants to tabernacle among and with mankind. God wants to have someone He can commit His oracles.

The leaders whom God calls, stand for His revealed character so we may learn to know Him more intimately. They stand so we may easily understand and apply by understanding God's character to our varied experiences. Leaders are to help us trust God more intelligently in our Christian growth.

God appeared unto Moses with the following:

> *I am Jehovah, the God of deliverance. Abraham never knew Me as a mighty deliverer, but as a leader, shepherd, protector and preserver. But you shall know Me as the God of deliverance. I am Jehovah. I have surely seen the affliction of My people which are in Egypt*

*and I have heard their cry by reason of their taskmasters, bondage, and lives made bitter by their oppressors. For I know their sorrows and I am come down to deliver them out of the hand of the Egyptians, and to bring them up out of that land unto a good land, flowing with milk and honey.*

Here, Almighty God shows Himself as the source where man can always come to find help in the time of need. God first shows to the leader and then to mankind what He really is. How big He is. That He is the God that inhabits eternity. That nothing is too hard for God. That He is interested in every microscopic detail of our lives. There is no place man can go except he finds God there. Psalm 139:7-8 says *"Whither shall I go from thy Spirit? or whither shall I flee from thy presence? If I ascend up into heaven, thou art there: if I make my bed in hell, behold, thou art there."*

God put a rod in Moses' hand and told him to return into Egypt and to show them His power. He told Moses to say unto Pharaoh, "Let My people go." This stick in the hand of God's leader was an emblem of authority from God. It revealed God's resistless power -- power that's unbinding and irresistible.

As the rod of God was the authority for Moses to deliver 6,000,000 Israelites out of bondage and the slave market of oppression, so is the Word of God to the leader. It is the sword of the Spirit. The Word of God is committed to God's

86

leader. It is the sword of the Spirit. The Word of God is committed to God's leader, in the power of the Holy Ghost, to deliver men from sin, sickness and oppression. These are the works of satan.

The normal business of a leader in all actuality, is to suffer for the cause of Christ or to be tested. Every leader must be willing to take his share of suffering. Suffering is expected of every good leader of Christ. Suffering, a force of the call to the ministry, is a call to a fellowship of suffering. It is these virtues which are transferred to the realm of the spirit in the phrase "a good solider of Jesus Christ."

## The Leader As A Teacher

Paul draws inevitable conclusions from facts which he writes in II Timothy 2:2-3. Paul pleads for the succession of teachers to pass on Christian knowledge from generation-to-generation. It reminds us of runners in a relay race who pass on the torch. He points out that there is a logical basis for prayer, sacrificial Christian service, courage, endurance and preaching, but also for teachers. Paul's conclusions state that christian teachers are to be willing to learn what is committed to them. Second, they must be faithful. Third, they must be able. Fourth, they must be concerned about others.

Three metaphors follow in quick succession as illustrations of what it means to be a Christian teacher. They are like a solider, he must be ready to endure hardships. Like an athlete, a Christian must keep the rules. Like a farmer, the Christian must work hard if he is to get results.

The following example will help you to understand how God chose one of His leaders. It will show you the quality and view of his acceptance and experience as a God-called leader.

## Gideon

*Gideon* had trouble believing in his own importance. Gideon saw nothing in himself that would recommend him to God, especially since he was no military man and Israel clearly needed a warrior against the Midianites. His interest was saving Israel.

Gideon's initial observation was look at my clan. He then said his clan was the weakest in Manasseh. He also felt he was the least in his father's family. However, Gideon was God's choice.

Gideon in the Hebrew means "hewer or grim warrior." His call came when he entertained God or His angel unawares. Gideon's call was substantiated, as he portrayed his loyalty to Yahweh by destroying his family and community's Baal altar. This call was later verified by the sign of the wet and dry fleece.

It seemed unlikely that God would take this unknown, outspoken, wheat-thresher and depend upon him for leadership. Yet, Gideon was given the important promise, "I will be with you." God made Gideon his person for the moment. Because Gideon knew who was directing his enterprise, it was clear in Judges 9, that Gideon could not be king. He could not take the glory. Gideon realized who the victor was. He knew who had really saved them.

This is the point of the Gideon story. God calls His leader. God imparts vision to His leader. God enables the leader to rule and obtain immeasurable success.

We will develop many strategies and use them to help us get the job done. However, our need is to understand that God is and will be working out His purpose for us. God works out His purpose for us in His own way and in His own time.

# SECTION II

# BLACK RELIGIOUS DENOMINATIONS IN AMERICA

## *CHAPTER 10*
## *BLACK DENOMINATIONS --*
## *THEIR ORIGINS AND BELIEFS*

## METHODISM

John Wesley is considered the founder of Methodism and was adamantly opposed to slavery. Bishop Francis Asbury is called the "Father of American Methodism." He, too, was opposed to slavery. Often, he grieved over the evil of slavery in America. Thus, he had a special compassion and burden for its oppressed victims. Bishop Asbury sought to help Black people.

Probably the greatest testament of Bishop Asbury's commitment to help Blacks is a story about a Black slave, named Punch, who was fishing on the bank of a stream. Bishop Asbury was traveling on a South Carolina highway when he stopped to talk with this slave. Bishop Asbury stopped his horse and went to sit by the slave's side for a conversation. He questioned the slave about whether he prayed. The slave responded that he did not. Bishop Asbury led the slave to the Lord, sang a hymn, and gave him some instructions and an exhortation. Twenty years and some sixty miles later, Punch came to thank Bishop Asbury for his instructions and conversion.

Bishop Francis Asbury

Francis Asbury was appointed forty-eight years later to a plantation mission that had approximately 200-300 slaves. He came upon one slave and asked if there was a preacher on the premises. The slaves said that there was an anointed preacher on the plantation, who stirred the hearts of the slaves. The slave said that crowds would gather around this preacher's cabin for prayer and exhortation. However, the slave preacher was only allowed to do so privately and in his own quarters. When the slave pointed Bishop Asbury to the preacher, Asbury was astonished to see that it was Punch. Asbury's gesture had given birth to an apostle who was leading a Black race of people to the Lord.

Bishop Asbury preached at the now infamous St. George's Church in Philadelphia, Pennsylvania. In 1769, the Methodists bought this church, unfinished, with four walls and a roof for about $1,000. Philadelphia's St. George's Methodist Episcopal Church is America's first Methodist church. Today, it is the world's oldest Methodist church in continuous service. Historically, St. George's Church would become a landmark for the evolution of the first Black church denomination in America.

St. George's Church sign

## African Methodist Episcopal Church

Richard Allen was born in 1760. When he was born, Allen's parents and their other children were slaves to the Philadelphia household of Benjamin Chew. The Allen family's responsibilities to the Chews' were to clean, cook and look after the Chews' five children. Later, when Richard was seven, his entire family was sold to Stokeley Sturgis. There, Allen and his family were brought up in Delaware, on a farm near Dover. At age 17, Sturgis eventually sold Richard's mother and three of her children to another family. He never saw his mother or the other children again.

Circuit preachers were very prominent during Allen's days. During that time, Blacks were forbidden to be with other Blacks unless a white person was present. However, one circuit preacher, named Gray, led Richard Allen to the Lord in 1777. This redemption offered Allen hope, personal discipline and responsibility. Allen, most of all, loved the fiery nature of the circuit preachers. Allen, himself, began preaching in 1780.

Richard Allen was gifted at convincing people. This gift would later help him attain his freedom from being a slave. Specifically, Allen used this gift on Master Sturgis by convincing him that Christianity made slaves better workers. By doing so, Allen convinced Sturgis to have Reverend Garrettson to come and preach on Sturgis' farm. Garrettson, a white man, preached against slavery. That day, Sturgis became so convicted that he decided to free Allen. The agreement was to allow Richard Allen to buy his own freedom for $2,000.

Richard Allen

Allen worked many nights and off-hours cutting cord wood and doing odd jobs. At the age of 20, Richard Allen bought his freedom. In 1786, he returned to the city of his birth.

Richard Allen was attracted to Methodism because of John Wesley's stand against slavery. He felt that Methodism offered the abolition of slavery, the conversion of Black people, discipline, and an easy to understand doctrine. This, Allen felt, would help Blacks to worship God freely and would allow them to use extemporaneous preaching. Richard Allen was a magnificent orator who specialized in extemporaneous preaching.

As a persuasive and magnificent speaker, Richard Allen's oratorical skills made him a regular at the St. George's Episcopal Church. So much so, that Allen began preaching regularly at St. George's 5:00 a.m. services. After the

Sunday morning services, he would then go out to preach three to four more sermons at different churches.

Allen's preaching attracted many Blacks. Year after year, the Black membership grew tremendously at St. George's. The white elders at St. George's became disturbed and concerned because many Blacks began supporting Allen in great numbers. They felt that it would be wise to assign these worshipers to segregated seats along the walls so they could be better controlled. These Black inspired worshipers met with severe opposition from the elders who placed further unnecessary restrictions upon them. Interracial tensions began to increase.

Allen asked the white elders at St. George's twice if he could start a Black church. Within a year of each request, Allen was denied both times. To

Absalom Jones

counteract the harmful influence that St. George's was having, Allen and Absalom Jones formed the Free African Society, a first toward organizing social life. The organization helped to teach Blacks about saving their finances, providing aid to the widowed, sick and jobless, and to help Black people help themselves. They also sought to improve morals among their brethren.

The increased numbers of Blacks that had joined St. George's Church eventually helped to create a need for a building expansion program. Black church members were tricked into funding the construction of

St. George's Methodist Episcopal
Church (before renovations)

the new church gallery. Their excitement toward participating in the building program would soon be thwarted. They soon found out that their money was used to build the upper galley, where they were now to be seated during the worship services.

One November Sunday in 1787, Richard Allen, Absalom Jones, and William White were ushered to the new galley by a white sexton. Because they arrived at the church late, they took their normal seats in the lower galley. While they were on their knees praying and worshiping God, a group of white men pulled Absalom Jones and the others up off their knees. The group of white men tried to force them to sit in the "assigned" seats. When the prayer was over and in a vote of thanks, confidence and commitment, Rev. Allen marched out of the church. Simultaneously, he said, "we will leave here and we will never be back." True to his commitment, Rev. Allen, Rev. Absalom Jones and his entourage walked out and never returned.

Meanwhile, the Free African Society under the leadership of Absalom Jones voted to draw up plans for the nation's first Black church. Robert Ralston, Benjamin Rush, and the Bishop of the Episcopal Church supported the church project both financially and morally. Richard Allen bought the land for the church, at 6th and Lombard in Philadelphia, out of his money.

Groundbreaking ceremonies took place in 1791 and Allen broke ground for the new church. Reverend Dickins of St. George's Church suggested Allen name the new church Bethel. Bethel means "house of the Lord." Three years later, on July 29, 1794, Bishop Asbury presided over the church's dedication.

Mother Bethel AME Church

The new church was able to use Methodist in its name. Allen felt that Methodism offered simplicity of the gospel and orderliness of rules and regulations. He felt that this was the most effective way to have Blacks gain an understanding and knowledge of the purposes of the Church. On the other hand, the Free African Society voted the use of Episcopalian in its name as well. In 1816, a court case recognized Bethel's right to exist as an independent denomination.

Later in their church development, the Bethelites refused to participate in the Methodist conference. White people then attempted to control the newly formed denomination. The whites sued the organization when they were refused preaching engagements at the church. The suit was unsuccessful because the Supreme Court ruled that Bethel was free to control their own religious affairs. The Court also ruled that Bethel was free to deny whites the right to preach or participate in their ceremonies.

Bethel's membership grew from 20 to 121 in two years. At some point, the basement of Bethel was used as a stop on the Underground Railroad. Sarah Allen helped with the Underground movement by hiding, feeding and clothing escaped slaves. Further, Sarah Allen is the first female missionary of the African Methodist Episcopal Church.

Sarah Allen

On April 9, 1816, Allen called together several Black Methodist Episcopal churches to a conference in Philadelphia. First, Allen wanted to use this conference as a chance to unite these churches as one body under the name of the African Methodist Episcopal Church of the United States. Second, he wanted to use the book of discipline of the Methodist Episcopal Church as their discipline. Therefore, Bethel Church became Bethel African Methodist Episcopal Church. The new denomination would adopt the episcopal form of church government. Allen believed this would allow the new denomination to be under the authority of bishops who were ordained by officials within the denomination. At the conference, Bishop Francis Asbury ordained Richard Allen as the first bishop over the formally organized African Methodist Episcopal Church. Richard Allen died on March 26, 1831.

The doctrinal beliefs of this organization are strictly Methodist. The church believes in the Trinity, regeneration and repentance, freedom of the will and justification by faith. They also believe in sanctification and holiness, the second coming of Jesus Christ and the enabling grace of God for perfection.

# African Methodist Episcopal Zion Church

A small group of Black church members protested against the discrimination they were receiving at John Street Methodist Church in New York City. Black members of John Street had been denied the sacraments and full participation at the church. In October 1796, under the leadership of James Varick, a group of Blacks sought out to start the African Methodist Episcopal Zion Church.

James Varick and others petitioned Bishop Francis Asbury for permission to meet among themselves. A series of meetings pursued at Varick's home. In August 1796, Bishop Asbury approved for them to hold separate meetings. They in turn rented a meeting house. This was the

Bishop James Varick

Mother AME Zion Church

beginning for the African Methodist Episcopal Zion Church.

The charter, however, was under the name of the African Methodist Episcopal Church and took place in New York City on April 6, 1801. The African Methodist Episcopal Zion Church's officials separated their ties with the Methodist church in 1821. In 1848, the General Conference voted to add "Zion" to the church's name. By adding "Zion" to the denomination's name, this distinguished them from the denomination started by Richard Allen.

The doctrinal beliefs of this organization are Methodist.

# Christian Methodist Episcopal Church

When the general conference of the Methodist Episcopal Church of the South met in 1866, Blacks requested that they be allowed to have their own church. The issue hwere wsa over slavery and the importance of Blacks participating in the Methodist Church's services. The conference granted the request under friendly terms.

In 1870, a committee was commissioned to study whether Blacks should be allowed to be a separate group instead of a subordinated group. They returned with and made a favorable recommendation. The committee recommended that, after the Civil War, Blacks should be allowed their independence and given the ability to participate in the social reconstruction of American society. As a result of this recommendation, Blacks established the Colored Methodist Episcopal Church. Further, an agreement between the separating parties was made. The name was changed from the "Colored Methodist Episcopal Church," in 1954, to the Christian Methodist Episcopal Church.

The doctrinal beliefs of this denomination are Methodist.

# Free Christian Zion Church of Christ

A small group of Black Methodist and Baptist preachers, led by E.D. Brown, founded this denomination in Redemption, Arkansas, on July 10, 1905. Free Christian Zion Church of Christ was developed because of a disbelief in making the church support any ecclesiastical organization. Leaders of this organization believed that taking care of the needy should be the primary responsibility of the Church.

The doctrinal beliefs of this organization are Methodist.

## Reformed Methodist Union Episcopal Church

A dispute arose over the election of ministerial delegates to the general conference. The outcome from the dispute ended with the group withdrawing from the African Methodist Episcopal Church in 1885, in Charleston, South Carolina. The first elected minister was William E. Johnson. The group subsequently formed the Reformed Methodist Union Episcopal Church.

The doctrinal beliefs are of the Methodist Episcopal Church of the South.

## Reformed Zion Union Apostolic Church

James R. Howell was a minister of the African Methodist Episcopal Church in New York. In April 1869, he left as a protest against discrimination by whites and the ecclesiasticism of other Black Methodist churches. Former members of the African Methodist Episcopal Church who were interested in holiness and Christian unity met in Boydton, Virginia, to form this organization.

In 1874, Reverend Howell became the bishop of the Church. The Reformed Zion Union Apostolic Church was originally known as the Zion Union Apostolic Church. The church was reorganized in 1881-1882 after internal friction disrupted in the church about Howell being made bishop.

The doctrinal beliefs are of the parent company, the Methodist Episcopal Church of the South.

## Union American Methodist Episcopal Church

In 1805, a group of forty dissatisfied members, led by Peter Spencer and William Anderson, left Asbury Methodist Church in Wilmington, Delaware, because of discrimination. Black members of Asbury felt they had been denied rites of the Church. This group formed the Ezion Methodist Episcopal Church. However, a dispute arose and Blacks left the Church and began worshiping outdoors and in private homes until 1813.

In 1813, the members joined forces and became an independent Methodist Church. They later bought a piece of property, from a Quaker, and established and incorporated this denomination three years before Richard Allen's African Methodist Episcopal Church.

The Union American Methodist Episcopal Church was originally incorporated as the Union Church of Africans. Defections from the membership to form the African Union Church forced this body to change the name to what it is presently called.

The doctrinal beliefs are of the parent company, the Methodist Episcopal Church of the South.

# Table 1
## TIMELINE FOR BLACK METHODIST CHURCHES

| Unknown | 1760 | 1769 | 1786 | 1787 |
|---|---|---|---|---|
| Bishop Francis Asbury gives birth to a black apostle named Punch | Richard Allen is born | Methodists buy the historical and infamous St. George's Episcopal Church in Philadelphia, Pennsylvania | Richard Allen returns to Philadelphia, Pennsylvania, a free man | On a November Sunday morning, a disruption occurs at St. George's Church - Richard Allen and others leave forever |

| 1791 | 1794 | 1796 | 1801 | 1805 |
|---|---|---|---|---|
| Groundbreaking ceremony for America's first Black church takes place | On July 29, Bishop Asbury officiates the ceremony of America's first Black church | In August, James Varick and other Black pari-shioners leave John Street Methodist Church in New York City to protest discrimination - Bishop Asbury approves their meeting separately<br><br>In October, James Varick starts the African Methodist Episcopal Zion Church denomination | On April 6, the African Methodist Episcopal Church, under Bishop James Varick is chartered | A group of 40 Black dissatisfied members, led by Peter Spencer and William Anderson, leave Asbury Methodist Church in Wilmington, DE - they formed the Ezion Methodist Episcopal Church |

| 1813 | 1816 | 1821 | 1848 | 1866 |
|---|---|---|---|---|
| A split occurred at Ezion - Thirty congregations left to form one organization while twenty-four congregations continued as the Union Church of Africans - the name was later changed to Union American Methodist Episcopal Church | A court recognizes Bethel's right to exist as an independent organization and to deny whites the right to preach at their churches<br><br>On April 9, Richard Allen calls Black Episcopal churches together to form the African Methodist Episcopal denomination | African Methodist Episcopal Zion Church separates ties from the Methodist Church | "Zion" is added to the African Methodist Episcopal Church, under Bishop Varick, to show the difference from Richard Allen's denomination | Blacks request to start their own church at the Methodist Episcopal Church of the South's conference. The Colored Methodist Episcopal Church began |

# Table 1 *(Continued)*
## TIMELINE FOR BLACK METHODIST CHURCHES

| 1869 | 1870 | 1874 | 1885 | 1905 |
|------|------|------|------|------|
| In April, the Reformed Zion Union Apostolic Church is formed by James R. Howell. The church was reorganized between 1881-1882, after an internal dispute over Howell being made Bishop | A committee of the Methodist Episcopal Church of the South studied whether Blacks should be allowed to have their own denomination. Their findings indicated that after the Civil War, the Methodist Episcopal Church of the South should agree to let Blacks start their own churches | James R. Howell becomes Bishop of the Reformed Zion Union Apostolic Church | Reformed Methodist Union Episcopal Church is formed in Charleston, South Carolina. The first pastor was William E. Johnson | Free Christian Zion Church of Christ is started by E.D. Brown and a group of Black Methodist and Baptist preachers, in Redemption, Arkansas |

| 1954 |
|------|
| The name for the Colored Methodist Episcopal Church is changed from Colored to "Christian" |

105

# BAPTIST

Roger Williams

Roger Williams is credited with founding the first Baptist church on American soil. Williams graduated from Cambridge University in 1627 and was ordained in the Church of England. Roger Williams decided to leave England after embracing the "Separatists" ideas because he was dissatisfied with the Puritan theocracy. Williams felt there should be a separation of church and state, and that every man should have an individual responsibility to God. In 1631, Williams arrived in Boston.

Despite Williams' separatist's views, he was made the pastor of a church in Salem. However, he was later banished from the colony because the Puritans did not embrace his beliefs. When Williams left Salem, he went to live for a short time in Plymouth. Shortly after that, Williams purchased land from some Indians in 1638 in Providence, Rhode Island. There, a colony was

First Baptist Church of U.S. soil

formed from some of his former church members from Salem. Charles II gave the new colony a royal charter in 1663. More important, this government's origin was used to grant religious freedom -- the first ever in world history. Afterwards, Williams established the first Baptist church in March, 1639. The new colony then called themselves Baptists because they felt it best described them.

Many Blacks joined the Baptist denomination because there was less formality, ritualism and more freedom of the local congregation. Attendance at Black Baptist churches was high due to the freedom of expression from the pastor and parishioners. For example, slave owners frequently liberated Black ministers to hold worship services in their own meeting houses. The Black Baptist church was allowed to operate with an absolute autonomy of the local congreation, arrange its own worship, and examine and baptize its own members.

The doctrinal beliefs of this organization are predicated upon the Bible as the sole rule for life, the Lordship of Jesus Christ and individual access to God. They believe in salvation through faith, local church independence, separation of church and state and the second coming of Jesus Christ.

## First Bryan-First African Baptist Church

A year before the War of Independence from Britain, in 1774, the first organized Black Baptist Church was founded. The pastor was a slave named David George. He inherited this small church in Silver Bluff, South Carolina, from a white preacher named Palmer. Eight slaves from the Galphin plantation were his first congregants.

Another Black pioneer preacher was George Liele, a former slave. Before the British Army could reach Gorge, Liele started the Yama Craw Baptist Church near Savannah, Georgia. George Liele had many disciples. One notable disciple was Andrew Bryan.

Andrew Bryan began preaching while a slave in Chatham County. In 1788, he purchased his freedom and formed a Black congregation. Bryan named his church the First Bryan Baptist Church and it was chartered under the same. Later, Bryan was put in prison for naming and chartering the church. His congregation was also whipped and beaten by neighboring whites because of the church's charter.

The First Bryan Baptist Church was very involved in the Black community affairs of those who lived in Savannah. In 1793, Bryan bought property for the First Bryan Baptist Church. Through the efforts of a White slave owner named Abraham Mar-shall, two Black slaves named Jesse Peter and Andrew Bryan became the first pastors of the First African Baptist Church. The church was constructed in 1873 and still stands.

First African Baptist Church
Savannah, GA

A dispute arose in 1832 over the doctrine and caused a schism. This resulted in two congregations -- the First Bryan Baptist Church and the First African Baptist Church. However, the congregations finally joined to become the First African Baptist Church. Both are, according to history records, direct descendants of Bryan's original congregation.

Several Black Baptist churches were organized afterwards and followed the pattern established by the First African Baptist Church. These Black Baptist churches were organized in the following cities and years: Petersburg, Virginia, 1776, Richmond, Virginia, 1780, Williamsburg, Virginia, 1785 and Lexington, Kentucky, 1790. The church's doctrinal beliefs are Baptist.

## Full Gospel Baptist Fellowship

Bishop Paul Morton, Sr. is the pastor of the Greater St. Stephens Baptist Church, with over 10,000 members, in New Orleans, Louisiana. In 1992, Bishop Morton felt the need to lead the charge to change a generation. The evidence is now called the Full Gospel Baptist Fellowship. In five years, Bishop Morton has amassed several pastors who represent over 100,000 constituents. These constituents include thousands of Christians and Christian leaders. The primary thrust for the Fellowship is to build, develop and discipline the mind. Use of the media are also key factors toward achieving their mission objectives.

Despite the criticisms, misrepresentations and scorn, Bishop Morton has stood as a giant against the national religious landscape to usher in a progressive revolutionary movement in the Black Baptist experience. The Full Gospel Baptist Fellowship uses a seven-tier leadership platform. This includes the bishop's council, the auxiliary council, state overseers, general overseers, district overseers, elder's council and state adjutants.

The doctrinal beliefs are a mixture of Baptist with a Pentecostal experience.

# General Association of Baptists in Kentucky

On August 16, 1865, in Louisville, Kentucky, twelve members from several churches decided to meet. They gathered at the Fifth Street Baptist Church and the General Association of Baptists in Kentucky was formed. The organization later purchased their first piece of property on August 21, 1866.

The doctrinal beliefs are Baptist. They support Christian education, missions, sound doctrine and stewardship.

# Lott Carey Baptist Foreign Mission Convention

On January 16, 1821, Reverend Carey went to West Africa as a missionary. Reverend Lott Carey is the first Black Baptist American missionary to Africa. A former slave, Lott Carey was born and raised a slave near Richmond, Virginia. In December 1821, at the Shiloh Baptist Church in Washington, D.C., several prominent ministers gathered to form this convention. There, the Lott Carey Baptist Foreign Mission Convention was formed and named after Reverend Lott Carey.

The Lott Carey Baptist Foreign Mission Convention supports over a hundred missionaries in several foreign countries. It is the only distinct missionary convention in the United States and is supported largely by Baptist churches, associations and state organizations. It supports evangelism, education, feeding the hungry and providing medical assistance to the needy.

## National Baptist Convention of America, Inc.

Historically, the National Baptist Convention of America has its beginnings from three conventions. They are the Baptist Foreign Mission Convention, the American National Baptist Convention and the National Baptist Educational Convention.

The Baptist Foreign Mission Convention was formed on November 24, 1880, in Montgomery, Alabama. In 1886, the American National Baptist Convention was formed in St. Louis, Missouri. In 1893, the National Baptist Educational Convention was founded in Washington, D.C. On September 28, 1895, in Atlanta, Georgia, these three conventions decided to formally merge. The merger formed the National Baptist Convention of America.

## National Baptist Convention, U.S.A., Inc.

The National Baptist Convention is said to have evolved out of the merger of the National Baptist Convention of America in 1895. (See National Baptist Convention of America.) The merger of the three conventions into the National Baptist Convention eventually became intricate parts of the now National Baptist Convention, U.S.A., Inc. The Baptist Foreign Mission Convention became the National Baptist Foreign Mission Board. The American National Baptist Convention became the Home Mission Board. The National Baptist Educational Convention continued and is called the Educational Board.

## National Primitive Baptist Convention, U.S.A.

Several Black ministers decided to meet who felt the call for Black clergy to unite. In Huntsville, Alabama, in 1907, Elders Clarence Sams, George Crawford, and James H. Carey came together to discuss forming a national convention. At the meeting, eighty-seven elders from seven southern states met and organized the National Primitive Baptist Convention.

## New England State Convention of Maine, New Hampshire, Rhode Island

On May 16, 1874, the New England State Convention of Maine, New Hampshire, Rhode Island was formed by nine pastors. The meeting took place at the Congdon Street Baptist Church in Rhode Island in Providence, Rhode Island. The founding nine pastors met to help support missionary and benevolent work, establish educational institutions, help Blacks leaving the South and to establish churches and parsonages.

The founding pastors for the Convention, who are recorded in history, are as follows: Horatio Carter, Rufus Perry, William Dixon, Robert Wynn, Doughty Miller, Joseph Johnson, George Tucker, Henry Thomas and William Holloway. The New England State Convention of Maine, New Hampshire, Rhode Island is considered to be the oldest Black Baptist organization in the United States.

# Pentecostal Free-Will Baptist Church, Inc.

In 1959, three Free-Will Baptist Churches began to merge. They joined themselves, in North Carolina, to form the Pentecostal Free-Will Baptist Church, Inc.

The doctrinal beliefs are a mixture of Baptist and Pentecostal beliefs. They include regeneration through faith in the blood of Jesus, sanctification, baptism of the Holy Spirit with the evidence of speaking in tongues, divine healing and the second coming of Jesus Christ.

# Progressive National Baptist Convention, Inc.

The issue over the tenure of the president of the Convention was a major issue for the National Baptist Convention, U.S.A. and the National Baptist Convention of America. It had been voted in 1922, that the tenure for any president serving the Convention would be limited to four years. However, the next president served for 18 years. When Dr. Jackson refused to step down after his four-year tenure, a disruption occurred. Two thousand delegates decided to vote to have Dr. Gardner Taylor voted in as President. Another issue then was whether the Convention should lend support to and have Dr. Martin Luther King, Jr. become a member of the Convention.

Dr. L.V. Booth, pastor of Zion Baptist Church in Cincinnati, Ohio, seized this opportunity. On September 11, 1961, Dr. Booth sent out a press release about a meeting at his church to start another convention. Thirty-three people came from fourteen states to the meeting and the Progressive National Baptist Convention was started.

## Table 2
## TIMELINE FOR BLACK BAPTIST CHURCHES

| 1631 | 1638 | 1639 | 1663 | 1774 |
|---|---|---|---|---|
| Roger Williams arrives in Boston, Massachu-setts | Roger Williams purchases land from Indians<br><br>A colony is formed from former church members | In March, Roger Williams starts the first Baptist church on American soil in Providence, Rhode Island | Charles II issues a royal charter - the charter is the first record of a religious group being granted religious freedom | David George starts the first organized Black Baptist Church, in Silver Bluff, South Carolina |

| 1788 | 1821 | 1865 | 1873 | 1874 |
|---|---|---|---|---|
| Andrew Bryan pur-chases his freedom - he is a disciple of George Liele, who was trained by David George<br><br>Andrew Bryan starts the first Black Baptist Church in Savannah, Georgia | On January 16, Rev. Lott Carey becomes the first Black Baptist Am-erican missionary to travel to Africa<br><br>Lott Carey Baptist Foreign Mission Convention is started at Shiloh Baptist Church, in Washing-ton, D.C. | On August 16, the General Associa-tion of Baptists in Kentucky starts in Louisville, Ken-tucky | The First African Baptist Church is built in Savannah, Georgia | On May 16, the first Black con-vention is started - the New England State Convention of Maine, New Hampshire, Rhode Island, in Providence, Rhode Island |

| 1880 | 1886 | 1893 | 1895 | 1907 |
|---|---|---|---|---|
| On November 24, the Baptist Foreign Mission Convention is started | American National Baptist Convention is started in St. Louis, Missouri | National Baptist Educational Convention is started in Washington, D.C. | On September 28, a merger takes place to form the National Baptist Convention of America in At-lanta, GA. A split eventually occurs<br><br>National Baptist Convention, U.S.A., Inc. is formed out of the September 28 meeting | National Primitive Baptist Convention, USA is started from the efforts of Elders Clarence Sams, George Crawford and James H. Carey in Huntsville, AL |

115

## Table 2 *(Continued)*
## TIMELINE FOR BLACK BAPTIST CHURCHES

| 1959 | 1961 | 1992 |
|------|------|------|
| Pentecostal Free-Will Baptist Church, in North Carolina, has its beginnings | On November 14-15, the Progressive National Baptist Convention is started in Cincinnati, Ohio | Bishop Paul Morton starts the Full Gospel Baptist Fellowship, in New Orleans, LA |

# DISCIPLES OF CHRIST

The roots of the Restoration Movement can be traced to the period after the Revolutionary War. Americans who had strong religious interests, had grown weary and tired of European theology and denominational barriers. As a result, Americans sought to change these by developing their own. From the late eighteenth century, the Restoration Movement produced three denominations known as the Churches of Christ in America. They are the Christian Church or the Disciples of Christ, the Independent Christian Churches and the Churches of Christ.

James O'Kelly withdrew from the Baltimore Methodist conference in 1793. O'Kelly left and asked others to join him, to form a church that would return to New Testament Christianity. History records show that almost seven thousand people joined him in his new movement, mostly in Virginia and North Carolina.

James O'Kelly

In 1802, a similar movement started among the Baptists in New England. Abner Jones and Elias Smith had difficulty excepting denominational methodologies and wanted religious simplicity. Jones and Smith felt that the Holy Bible should be a Chris-

Abner Jones

Elias Smith

117

tian's only source for living. They sought out to use only this methodology to start a New Testament work.

In 1804, in the western frontier state of Kentucky, Barton W. Stone and several other Presbyterian preachers took similar action. These preachers declared they would take the Bible as the only source for Christian living.

Thomas Campbell, and his son, Alexander, made a similar move in 1809. However, they were in what is now known as West Virginia. Both father and son felt that Christians should experience freedom in Christian worship. Doctrines, they believed, hindered responsible Christian living.

Thomas Campbell          Alexander Campbell

James O'Kelly, Abner Jones, Elias Smith and the Campbells came together to form this denomination. Though they came from different geographical regions, their common beliefs helped to bring independence from each into one movement. Initially, they did not join to start a denomination. Their objectives were to focus on Christian living according to the Bible. They were primarily interested in establishing a New Testament Church, such as the one on Pentecost, A.D. 30.

The doctrinal beliefs of this denomination include baptism by emersion, a capella singing, vigorous prayer life and support of the church through giving.

These fellowships focus on the divinity of Christ, receiving the Holy Spirit after conversion and the Bible as the inspired Word of God. Their beliefs also include future rewards and punishments and that God answers prayer.

## General Assembly Churches of Christ (Disciples of Christ)

In 1886, Joe Whitley, Bill Ant'ly, Offie Pettiford and Easom Green developed this denomination from what was initially known as the Disciples Church. Founders of this organization agreed with Alexander Campbell, son of Thomas Campbell, that the church should conform to the New Testament Church of the Bible. This meant taking on the title of "disciple," in the church's name. Although this is a spinoff of the white Christian Church (Disciples of Christ), it does function as an independent Black religious denomination.

The doctrinal beliefs of this organization are use of the sacraments, foot washing with Holy communion and water baptism.

# Table 3
## TIMELINE FOR BLACK DISCIPLE OF CHRIST CHURCHES

| 1793 | 1802 | 1804 | 1809 | 1871 |
|------|------|------|------|------|
| James O'Kelly withdraws from the Baltimore Methodist Conference to return to New Testament Christianity | Abner Jones and Elias Smith withdraw from the Baptist denomination, in New England, to return to New Testament Christianity | Barton W. Stone and other preachers withdraw from the Presbyterian denomination, in Kentucky, to form a "New Testa-ment" church | Thomas Campbell and his son Alexander venture out as "disciples," in West Virginia, to form a new denomination | The Church of Christ (Disciples of Christ) denomination is formed |

| 1886 | 1931 |
|------|------|
| Joe Whitley, Bill Ant'ly, Offie Pettiford, Easom Green start the first Black Disciples of Christ denomination - called the General Assembly of Churches of Christ (Disciples of Christ) | The Church's name was modified from "Church of Christ" to "Disciples of Christ" |

# ORTHODOX

The first Orthodox church in America was established in 1921 by Dr. George Alexander McGuire. An emigrant from Antigua to the United States, McGuire served as a priest in the Protestant Episcopal Church until 1918. Several discrimination incidents against McGuire and his fellow clergy played a major role in them severing ties with the Episcopal Church. McGuire felt it was imperative to start a Black denomination so that equality and spiritual freedom for Blacks could be achieved. He also felt that a Black denomination should be run by a Black administration. Thus, McGuire became associated with Marcus Garvey and Garvey's Universal Negro Improvement Association.

When George Alexander McGuire started the African Orthodox Church, Marcus Garvey supported him heavily through the print media. Garvey's periodical called, "The Negro World," published many articles on McGuire. This was especially true when McGuire was consecrated as bishop by Archbishop Joseph Rene Vilatte. Vilatte, of the American Catholic Church, was a white man who had suspicious credentials, nevertheless, McGuire felt it would do at the time. Archbishop Vilatte was also chosen because he did not seek to control or become involved in Bishop McGuire's denomination. George Alexander McGuire died in 1935.

The doctrinal beliefs of the Orthodox Church places a strong emphasis on the apostolic succession and historic sacraments and rituals. The Church uses the seven sacraments of the Roman Catholic Church and the blend of Western and

Eastern liturgy, creeds and symbols. Western and Eastern liturgical blends are usually mixed with Anglican, Greek and Roman patterns.

## African Orthodox Church

George Alexander McGuire felt that Black Episcopalians should have churches of their own. He withdrew from the Protestant Episcopalian Church in 1919 to start the African Orthodox denomination. George McGuire was ordained bishop of the African Orthodox churches in 1921.

The doctrinal beliefs of this denomination are Orthodox.

## Table 4
### TIMELINE FOR BLACK ORTHODOX CHURCHES

| 1918 | 1919 | 1921 |
|------|------|------|
| Dr. George A. McGuire, a former citizen of the West Indies, served as a priest in the Protestant Episcopal Church in Antiqua and the United States | As a result of several discrimination incidents, McGuire severes ties from the Episcopal Church and starts the African Orthodox denomination | On September 2, the African Orthodox Church was established at a meeting at the Church of the Good Shepherd, in New York City |
| | | On September 29, in the Church of the Lady of Good Death, in Chicago, Illinois, Dr. McGuire is ordained bishop of the African Orthodox Churches, by Archbishop Joseph Rene Vilatte |

# PENTECOSTAL/APOSTOLIC, HOLINESS AND DELIVERANCE

On New Year's Eve into the New Year of 1901, Charles Parham had a revival in Topeka, Kansas. A woman by the name of Agnes Ozman, who was attending the revival, began to speak in tongues. When others, who were present at the meeting witnessed what had happened, it had an unprecedented effect. From that time, Parham's revivals were followed by more of this experience. Later, however, Parham would be faced with major problems. In 1907, he was charged with committing sodomy with young adult males. By the 1910s, Charles Parham had become a full-fledged racist and a Klan supporter.

Prior to Parham's misfortunes, he traveled to Texas in 1904. William Seymour attended one of his services. Because Seymour was Black, he was not allowed to sit in the classroom. He was allowed to sit in the hallway of the building.

William Seymour

In 1905, over at the Second Baptist Church of Los Angeles, several members moved toward holiness approaches to salvation instead of the Baptist teachings. The group who supported this approach was ousted from the church. They, in turn, formed a church at 9th and Santa Fe. The exiles at the new church called William Seymour, in 1906, to pastor the new church. When Seymour got to

Los Angeles in February 1906, he raised the issue of speaking in tongues as the evidence of being filled with the Holy Spirit. Already facing controversial issues, the church group ousted Seymour.

At 214 N. Bonnie Brae Street, William Seymour held meetings at the home of Richard and Ruth Asberry, Baptist relatives of Neeley Terry. The meetings were interracial and lay people exercised leadership and special gifts. This would be a trademark of Seymour. During this time, Seymour was living in the home of Edward Lee.

On April 9, 1906, Edward Lee and Jennie Evans Moore began speaking in tongues. Many others also experienced the same and the community became stirred. As a result, Seymour rented an abandoned industrial building previously used by an African Methodist Episcopal Church. The building was at 312 Azusa Street and was called the Apostolic Faith Mission. Word of what was taking place at Azusa Street was spreading like wildfire because

312 Azusa Street

Seymour published a paper called the Apostolic Faith. He sent 50,000 copies of the paper out free of charge to subscribers.

By mid-May 1906, the church was filled. The Pentecostal movement had its beginnings. Within the year, many leaders from the Mission started numerous congregations. Some notable ones were the 51st Street Apostolic Faith Mission, the Spanish AFM and the Italian Pentecostal Mission. After Seymour's death, the Mission was still a large size. Jennie Moore, whom Seymour married in 1908, assumed the pastorate for a few years. However, the congregation disbanded after the church lost their building in 1931.

The Azusa Street revival weakened because of spiritual and social abuse. However, the Pentecostal movement had mushroomed into the Pacific Northwest and Southeast regions. Many capable leaders came out of the Azusa revival. One such leader was Charles Mason, founder of the Church of God in Christ denomination. Another was Howard Goss, one of the founders for the Assemblies of God.

Charles Mason had become the head of the Church of God in Christ before Azusa. Unlike William Seymour, Bishop Mason could ordain people as legitimate ministers by civil authorities and mainstream churches. Therefore, Charles Mason served as the primary source of ordinations for both Black and white Pentecostal and Holiness churches.

Charles Mason brought the Pentecostal experience back to his denomination. The experience was well received. Today, the Church of God in Christ is the largest Black Pentecostal denomination in America. On the other hand, Howard Goss and others decided to bring the Pentecostal experience to their local associations. Several people from the Baptist, Alliance and Holiness churches responded to his request. This group formed the Assemblies of God.

In 1898, Ambrose Blackmon Crumpler, a Methodist evangelist, had an uncompromising holiness ministry. His evangelistic ministry had a great influence in North Carolina. Thus, the first church to use the Pentecostal Holiness Church's name was organized in Goldsboro, North Carolina because of his ministry.

The Fire-Baptized Holiness Church was a result of Benjamin Hardin Irwin's evangelistic ministry. Irwin, a Nebraskan, was a Baptist lawyer. He later converted to the Wesleyan holiness theology. From 1896 to 1900, Irwin held revivals in the South and Midwest. Rejected from the National Holiness Movement, because of his teachings on "third blessingism," Irwin started the Fire-Baptized Holiness Associations. The first Association was started in Olmitz, Iowa in 1895, and has flourished throughout the nation.

The denomination's doctrinal beliefs include sanctification, speaking in tongues, expressive spiritual dancing and foot washing. The Church also theologically supports divine healing, holiness and the deity of Christ.

## Apostolic Faith Churches of God, Inc.

In 1909, under the leadership of Bishop William Seymour, the Apostolic Faith Churches of God developed out of the Azusa Street Revival. The church was founded by Bishop William Seymour and Charles W. Lowe. The work is headquartered in Franklin, Virginia, but the presiding bishop is Oree Keyes of Jefferson, Ohio.

The denomination's doctrinal beliefs include sanctification, speaking in tongues, expressive spiritual dancing and foot washing.

## Apostolic Faith Mission Church of God

F.W. Williams was part of the Azusa Pentecostal experience under Bishop William Seymour. On July 10, 1906, F.W. Williams founded the Apostolic Faith Mission Church of God. Afterwards, he returned to the South and started a Mississippi branch. There, he experienced opposition and the work was abandoned.

Williams then went to Mobile, Alabama, to conduct a revival at a Primitive Baptist church. The entire congregation at the Primitive Baptist church was converted through Williams' revival. Williams subsequently began pastoring the church. Later, he bought the church's building to become the new denomination's home.

Once Williams embraced the oneness doctrine of the Apostolic in 1915, he broke ties with Bishop Seymour. Consequently, he adopted the name of the Apostolic Faith Mission Church of God. The church was officially incorporated on October 9, 1915.

The doctrinal beliefs of this organization are Apostolic. The organization believes in healing and baptizes in the name of the Lord Jesus Christ. They also believe in foot washing during communion and women preachers.

## Apostolic Overcoming Holy Church of God

Bishop William Thomas Phillips, a former member of the Methodist Church, was rooted in the doctrine and teaching of holiness. He was convinced in 1912 that holiness was God's system. Bishop Phillips set out to organize the Ethiopian Overcoming Holy Church of God in 1916. Ethiopian was later changed to Apostolic when Bishop Williams wanted the title to reflect their embracing all races.

The denomination's doctrinal beliefs include sanctification, speaking in tongues, expressive spiritual dancing and foot washing. Theologically, they believe in divine healing, holiness, the deity of Christ and the second coming of Jesus Christ.

## Bible Way Church of Our Lord Jesus Christ World Wide, Inc.

Bible Way Church of Our Lord Jesus Christ World Wide, Inc. began after a concern about the unwillingness of Bishop Robert Lawson to appoint a board of bishops to help him. When Bishop Lawson refused to address these concerns at the thirty-eight Convocation, Elder Smallwood Williams and others left the Convocation and the denomination.

Elder Williams and other ministers came together at the National Pentecostal Ministerial Conference in Washington, D.C. in 1957. It was there that Williams and four others were made bishops. The Bible Way Church of Our

Lord Jesus Christ World Wide was then developed and is headquartered in Washington, D.C.

The denomination's beliefs are oneness and apostolic. They believe in baptism of the Holy Ghost with the evidence of speaking in tongues, divine healing, baptism in Jesus' name only and a Pentecostal theology.

## Churches of God, Holiness

Bishop King Hezekiah Buruss and eight other people set out in 1914, in Atlanta, Georgia, to start the Holiness Church of God. Bishop Buruss incorporated this denomination into what is now called the National Convention of the Churches of God, Holiness.

The doctrinal beliefs are predicated on the Holy Bible as God inspired, the Trinity, the gift of the Holy Spirit, the Lord's Supper and foot washing. Before membership into this denomination, each must believe in divine healing.

## Church of Christ (Holiness) U.S.A.

Charles Price Jones, a former Baptist member, left the Baptist fellowship because they did not support sanctification through the Holy Spirit. Jones left and started the Church of Christ Holiness in 1894 in Jackson, Mississippi. In 1898, the church became a full-fledged Holiness organization.

Charles Price Jones encouraged Charles Mason to attend the Azusa revival. When Mason returned, after receiving the baptism of the Holy Spirit, a strong disagreement occurred between Jones and Mason. Jones differed strongly with Mason that it was not necessary to speak with tongues as evidence of being filled with the Holy Spirit. Many followers of Bishop Mason left to form the Church of God in Christ. Charles Jones reorganized the Church of Christ Holiness according to the Holiness theology.

This denomination believes in the salvation through grace and baptism in Jesus' name only.

## Church of God and Saints of Christ

William S. Crowdy was a former Baptist deacon from Lawrence, Kansas. Crowdy left the Baptist Church to go on his own after receiving a special visitation from God. He believed that God had given him a vision and a commission to deliver God's prophetic truth to the world. Rev. Crowdy established the Church of God and Saints of Christ denomination in 1896.

The Church of God and Saints of Christ is a group of people who are occasionally called Black Jews, because they celebrate most of the Jewish holy and feast days. These Black Jews believe their church is built upon the patriarchs and prophets of the Jewish tradition.

The Church of God and Saints of Christ operates solely on the Decalogue.

# Church of God In Christ, Inc.

Bishop Charles Harrison Mason and Charles Price Jones were rejected by Baptist groups in Arkansas for what was considered as an overemphasis on holiness. They founded the Church of God In Christ, in Memphis, Tennessee, during the 1890's.

Mason met Charles Jones in Mississippi in 1895. Before then, Mason had been preaching on his own. When the two met, they started a revival in Jackson,

Bishop Charles Mason

Mississippi, in 1896. In 1897, at Lexington, Mississippi, the previous revival in Jackson led to a second revival. There, the Church of God in Christ was formally established. However, the Church was incorporated, in 1897, as a chartered denomination in Memphis, Tennessee. This denomination was the first Southern holiness denomination that became legally chartered.

The Church of God In Christ's doctrine is Trinitarian. They stress repentance, regeneration, justification, sanctification, speaking in tongues, and the gift of healing as evidence of the baptism of the Holy Spirit.

## Church of Our Lord Jesus Christ of the Apostolic Faith, Inc.

The Church of Our Lord Jesus Christ denomination was organized in 1919 by Robert Clarence Lawson in Columbus, Ohio. Lawson served under Bishop

Garfield Hayward, who served as pastor of a branch of the Pentecostal Assemblies of the World. Later, Lawson joined the Pentecostal Assemblies of the World and aided in starting churches in several states. Lawson believed that his denomination was a continuation of the great revival that began in Jerusalem on the day of Pentecost.

When Lawson refused to share his bishopric or divide the leadership within the church, a split occurred. In 1933, Sherrod C. Johnson was one of the ones who left the church to form his Church of the Lord Jesus Christ of the Apostolic Faith. Bishop Smallwood E. Williams also left the organization to form what is now known as the Bible Way Church of the Lord Jesus Christ. Bishop Henry C. Brooks was another who left Lawson's church. In 1927, Bishop Brooks started the Way of the Cross Church of Christ and wanted no organizational affiliations with Lawson's church.

The doctrinal beliefs of this organization include the priesthood of all believers, baptism by immersion and baptism of the Holy Spirit. The denomination also believes in foot washing, the resurrection and the second coming of Jesus.

## Fire-Baptized Holiness Church of the Americas

Formerly known as the Colored Fire Baptized Holiness Church, the Black membership of the white Pentecostal fire-baptized church separated in 1908. This organization was founded by Bishop and Sister W. E. Fuller. The church took its present name in 1922.

The Fire-Baptized Holiness Churches believe glorification of the body are wicked. Their doctrines include repentance, regeneration, justification and sanctification. They also believe in a Pentecostal baptism with the evidence of speaking in tongues, divine healing and the return of Jesus Christ.

## Pentecostal Assemblies of the World, Inc.

In 1906, there was an interracial body of believers in Los Angeles, California. Bishop Garfield Thomas Haywood, the first Black leader in the organization, advocated the "oneness" doctrine even to the other white leaders. However, the white members began withdrawing in 1924 to form the Pentecostal Church, Inc.

The doctrinal beliefs of this denomination are centered on holiness, sanctification, speaking in tongues and baptism in Jesus' name only.

## United Holy Church of America, Inc.

Method, North Carolina, was the scene for the emerging of this new Pentecostal church. In 1886, Isaac Cheshier, organized this body originally as the Holy Church of North Carolina. However, it was later changed to the United Holy Church of America, on September 25, 1918.

The United Holy Church of America's doctrines include beliefs in the Trinity, revelation of God in the Bible, redemption through Jesus Christ and justification through sanctification. Other doctrinal beliefs include baptism of the Holy Ghost, divine healing and the second coming of Jesus Christ.

# Table 5
## TIMELINE FOR BLACK PENTECOSTAL/APOSTOLIC/HOLINESS AND DELIVERANCE CHURCHES

| 1886 | 1896-1900 | 1894 | 1896 | 1897 |
|---|---|---|---|---|
| Isaac Cheshier starts the United Holy Church of America in Method, North Carolina | Benjamin Hardwin Irwin, a Nebraskan and a Baptist lawyer, started the fire-baptized holiness church. His ministry greatly influenced those in the South and Midwest regions. He also started the Fire-Baptized Holiness Associations in Olmitz, Iowa, a year earlier | Charles Price Jones starts the Church of Christ Holiness (USA) denomination in Jackson, Mississippi | The Church of God and Saints of Christ was started in Lawrence, Kansas, by William S. Crowdy | The Church of God In Christ denomination becomes the first holiness denomination to become legally chartered |

| 1898 | 1901 | 1904 | 1905 | 1906 |
|---|---|---|---|---|
| Ambrose Blackmon Crumpler, a Methodist evangelist, greatly influenced the religious arena in North Carolina. Thus, he had the first ministry to use the Pentecostal Holiness Church's name. This took place in Goldsboro, North Carolina | Charles Parham holds a revival where Agnes Ozman began to speak in tongues - many others had the same experience after Ms. Ozman's. The Pentecostal experience is said to revolve out of this event on a national basis | William Seymour travels to experience one of Charles Parham's pentecostal revivals | A group of members were ousted from Second Baptist Church because they insisted on moving toward holiness approaches to salvation instead of the Baptist teachings. This group would later ask William Seymour to pastor their newly found church | William Seymour began pastoring a new church that started from a group of members ousted from the Second Baptist Church. Seymour was later ousted because he raised the issue of speaking in tongues |

136

## Table 5 *(Continued)*
## TIMELINE FOR BLACK PENTECOSTAL/APOSTOLIC/HOLINESS
## AND DELIVERANCE CHURCHES

| 1906 (Continued) |
| --- |
| At 214 N. Bonnie Brae Street, William Seymour holds interracial meetings at the home of Richard and Ruth Asberry |
| Seymour moves his meetings from the Asberry's home into a rented and abandoned building at 312 Azusa Street |
| The Azusa Street revival begins to make history |
| The Pentecostal Assemblies of the World was started in Los Angeles, California, by Bishop Garfield Haywood |
| Only July 10, F.W. Williams starts the Apostolic Faith Mission Church of God, in Mobile, Alabama |

137

# Table 5 *(Continued)*
## TIMELINE FOR BLACK PENTECOSTAL/APOSTOLIC/HOLINESS AND DELIVERANCE CHURCHES

| 1908 | 1909 | 1914 | 1916 | 1919 |
|---|---|---|---|---|
| Bishop and Sister W.E. Fuller start the Fire-Baptized Holiness Church of the Americas | Bishop William Seymour and Charles W. Lowe start the Apostolic Faith Churches of God. The organization is headquartered in Franklin, Virginia | Bishop King Hezekiah Buruss, in Atlanta, Georgia, starts the Churches of God, Holiness. It is now called the National Convention of the Churches of God, Holiness | The Apostolic Overcoming Holy Church of God has its beginnings through the efforts of Bishop William Thomas Phillips. It was originally called the Ethiopian Overcoming Holy Church of God | Bishop Robert Clarence Lawson starts the Church of Our Lord Jesus Christ of the Apostolic Faith in Columbus, Ohio |
| William Seymour marries Jennie Moore, who takes over his Church after his death | | | | |

| 1957 |
|---|
| Bishop Smallwood E. Williams starts the Bible Way of Our Lord Jesus Christ World Wide denomination in Washington, D.C. |

138

# NONDENOMINATIONAL/CHARISMATIC

Charismatics, or the "New Pentecostals," are doctrinally similar to those from Protestant denominations and Azusa Street Pentecostalists. Charismatics primarily focus on the Holy Spirit or the Third Person in the Trinity. Through personal relationships with Jesus Christ, Charismatics promulgate their Christian experiences through Bible studies, worship, prayer and evangelistic witness.

The movement of Charismatics, theologically, was to personalize God. They felt God had always been deified as one whom we had to "practice good" to receive His favor. However, Charismatics sought to technically prove He was personable, loving and wanted an intimate relationship with people whom He created. Personalizing God, according to Charismatics, produces a radical people who can produce "fruit" from their practical and day-to-day living approaches to a "touchable" God.

The ecclesiastical methodology of Charismatics does not require public marketing to garner support for its theological stance. The significant propulsions of their beliefs are directed through "personalizing" the community with cell groups and fellowships. Attitudinal differences between Charismatics, mainline Protestants, and Pentecostals are the uses of localized parachurch groups. Growth patterns show their concentrated efforts toward building personal relationships with God, economic empowerment and educational achievements.

The major doctrinal distinctives of the Charismatic movement are the baptism in the Holy Spirit, prophecy, the gift of healing and the emphasis on having a personal relationship with God. They also embrace lay leadership, new incentives for evangelization, missions and witness in the power of the Spirit.

## Crenshaw Christian Center

Dr. Frederick K.C. Price had been involved with several denominations before becoming inspired by Kenneth Hagin's book on the "Authority of the Believer." Inspired and motivated by this new revelation, Dr. Price began teaching his West Washington Community Church congregation about the power of the Holy Spirit. Rapid church growth came because of his revelatory teachings. Concomitantly, several properties were purchased to hold the influx of people who were being empowered to prosper and grow through application of God's Word.

Popularity and interest in Dr. Price's teachings spread rapidly throughout the United States and abroad. Dr. Price's use of outreach ministries, the media, and crusades helped to influence the masses through God's Word to the masses. As a result, Dr. Price is considered one of the pioneer leaders of the "charismatic and faith movement" for minorities, especially Blacks.

Dr. Frederick K.C. Price pastors over 14,000 members at Crenshaw Christian Center Church in Los Angeles, California. Crenshaw Christian Center holds its services in the Faith Dome, the largest church sanctuary in the United States.

The Faith Dome, which opened Sunday, September 10, 1989, has a 10,145-seating capacity.

The doctrinal beliefs of this organization include baptism in the Holy Spirit and speaking in tongues as evidence of being filled with the Holy Spirit. They also believe in the use of God's Word as final authority.

## Azusa Interdenominational Fellowship of Christian Churches and Ministries

Bishop Carlton Pearson held the first Azusa Conference in April 1988, in the Johnson Theater quadrant of the ORU Mabee Center. The resurgence of the phenomenon that happened at the 1906 Azusa revival, again is making its mark in history.

With the last decade of a millennium nearing an end, Bishop Pearson sought to bring an interracial and interdenominational group of people together in a multicultural expression of love and worship. His focus was to transcend racial and cultural barriers by reminding them of what took place in 1906 on Azusa Street. In similar spirit, the Conference made great strides in assembling and preparing God's people for world evangelism.

The Azusa Interdenominational Fellowship of Christian Churches and Ministries was founded in 1993 as an outreach of the Azusa Conference. Over 2,000 ministers and pastors are associated with this organization. The objectives of the organization are to refine and develop ministries, help inner-city troubled youths and conduct marriage enrichment seminars. Other programs include ministerial licensing and ordination, fraternal accountability and worldwide evangelism through international Azusa conferences.

## Table 6
## TIMELINE FOR NONDENOMINATIONAL AND CHARISMATIC CHURCHES

| 1906 | 1973 | 1988 |
|------|------|------|
| William Seymour starts the Pentecostal movement in Los Angeles, California | Rev. Dr. Frederick K.C. Price leaves the Presbyterian, Baptist, African Methodist Episcopal and Christian Missionary Alliance denominations, to start Crenshaw Christian Center Church in Los Angeles, California | Bishop Carlton Pearson starts the Azusa Interdenominational Fellowship of Christian Churches and Ministries in Tulsa, Oklahoma |

# SECTION III

# A COMPREHENSIVE CHURCH DENOMINATION, ECUMENICAL AND SERVICE AGENCY MODEL

# AN ANALYSIS OF THE WASHINGTON, D.C. METROPOLITAN AREA BLACK CHURCH DENOMINATIONS

This section provides an analysis of black church denominations in the Washington, D.C. metropolitan area. The churches researched and surveyed for this book were taken from a 20 mile radius in the nation's capital. Included in the sampling was Washington, D.C., Maryland and Virginia. The sampling also included dividing each into subsections (i.e., N.E., N.W.). The subsections were then divided into denominations.

In the Washington, D.C. metropolitan area, there are 593 Black churches. The Black churches sampled for this book are Protestant in structure. The

Protestant category includes the Methodist, Baptist, Disciples of Christ, Pentecostal/Apostolic/Holiness/Deliverance and Nondenominational/Charismatic churches.

Twelve black church denominations are housed in the Washington, D.C. metropolitan area. They are African Methodist Episcopal (AME), Apostolic, Baptist, Christian Methodist Episcopal (CME) and Church of God In Christ (COGIC). In addition, Holiness, Nondenominational/Charismatic, Pentecostal, Pentecostal/Holiness, Disciples of Christ and the United Methodist (UM) churches are also listed.

Churches defined as Nondenominational are independent fellowships that are not affiliated with any major organization, nor are they known as major or leading denominations. Nondenominational churches are called Charismatic, Independent, Christian, Community, Full Gospel, Word, Faith, Interdenominational and Unity.

Figure 10 shows the ratio of churches per state, for the entire Washington, D.C. area. Washington, D.C. leads with 70.7% of the Black churches.

Part I of this Section provides a breakdown of the black church denominations by state. Graphic charts are also included in each section's listing, to help decipher the ratio significance of churches concentrated in any one particular area. Part II of this Section lists the names and addresses of churches in the Washington, D.C., Maryland and Virginia areas. Part III provides the names and addresses of ecumenical organizations and service agencies.

146

## Figure 10
## Geographical Concentration of Churches

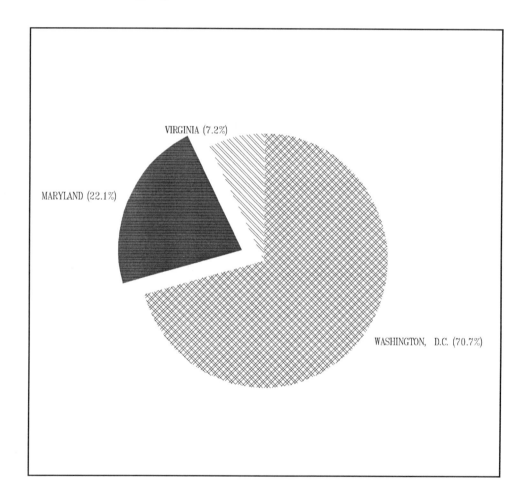

---

## PART I
## DENOMINATIONAL BREAKDOWN OF
## WASHINGTON D.C. 'S BLACK CHURCHES

## WASHINGTON, D.C.

Washington, D.C. has 418 Black churches. Out of this number, 147 churches are located in the northeast and 170 in the northwest. Ninety-six (96) are located in the southeast and 5 are in the southwest section.

The data in Table 7 and Figure 11 shows that the Baptist denomination has 58% of the churches. It is the leading form of religion in Washington, D.C. area.

The Holiness denomination ranks second and the Nondenominational churches are ranked third. The United Methodist and Apostolic churches rank fourth and fifth respectfully, while the Pentecostal/Holiness churches rank sixth. The

## Table 7 - Number of Churches Per Denomination

| | |
|---|---|
| African Methodist Episcopal (AME) | ( 16) |
| Apostolic | ( 20) |
| Baptist | (232) |
| Christian Methodist Episcopal (CME) | ( 5) |
| Church of God In Christ (COGIC) | ( 16) |
| Disciples of Christ | ( 3) |
| Holiness | ( 48) |
| Nondenominational | ( 32) |
| Pentecostal | ( 19) |
| Pentecostal/Holiness | ( 2) |
| United Methodist (UM) | ( 23) |

## Figure 11
## Denominational Percent of Churches for Washington, D.C.

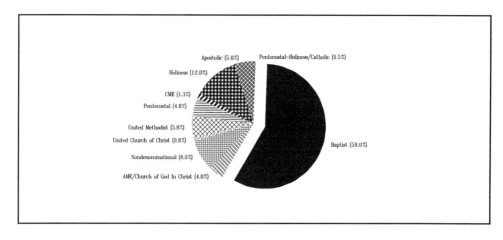

Church of God In Christ and the African Methodist Episcopal churches are both ranked seventh and the Christian Methodist Episcopal churches are ranked eighth. The United Church of Christ churches rank ninth, while the Pentecostal/Holiness churches each have the same percentages and are ranked tenth.

The data in Figure 12 shows the denominational relationship of churches in the northeast section of Washington, D.C. Figures 13-15 also show the denominational relationship of churches in the northwest, southwest and southeast sections of Washington, D.C. Following each figure is a list of churches per denomination for the northeast, northwest, southeast and southwest sections of Washington, D.C.

## Figure 12
## Denominational Percent of N.E. Churches

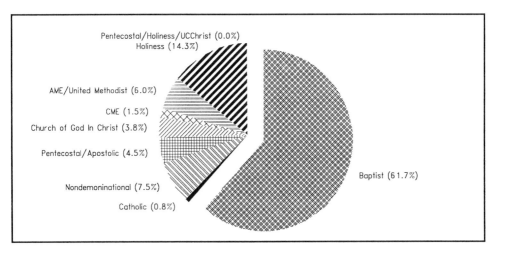

# WASHINGTON, D.C. NORTHEAST SECTION - 147 churches

African Methodist Episcopal (AME) (8)    -   Beth Shalom AME Zion Church
Brown Memorial AME Church
Contee Mae AME Zion
Pilgrim AME Church
Reid Temple AME Church
Union Wesley AME Zion Church
Varick Memorial AME Zion Church
Ward Memorial AME Church

Apostolic (6)    -   Church of the Lord Jesus Christ of
     of the Apostolic Faith
Grace Temple Bibleway
Miracle from God Apostolic Church
Straitegate Bibleway Church
Way of the Cross Church of Christ
Whole Truth Church of the
     Lord Jesus Christ

Baptist (82)    -   Antioch BC
Bethesda BC
Beulah BC of Deanwood Heights
Bible BC
Brookland Union BC
Central Union BC
Charity BC
Christian Love BC
Congregational Primitive BC
Daughter of Zion BC
Deutoronomy Missionary BC
Divine Love BC
East Friendship BC
Ebenezer BC
Enon BC

Baptist (Continued)

Evergreen BC
Fellowship BC
First BC of Deanwood
First Jericho BC
First New Hope BC
Friendly Memorial BC
Galatians BC
Glendale BC
Greater Friendly BC
Greater Mount Zion BC
Greater Mt. Pisgah BC
Greater Pleasant Grove BC
Greater Victory BC
Guiding Star BC
Guildfield BC
Holy Trinity Missionary BC
Holyway BC
Isle of Patmos BC
Israel BC
James Memorial BC
Jericho BC
Kingdom of Zion BC
Mount Jezreel BC
Mount Siloam BC
Mt. Airy BC
Mt. Horeb BC
Mt. Olive BC
New Birth Missionary BC
New Birth Prayer Missionary BC
New Canaan BC
New Covenant BC
New Genesis BC
New Horizon BC
New Life BC

Baptist (Continued)

New Light Missionary BC
New Mount Calvary BC
New Mount Olive BC
New Samaritan BC
New St. John Missionary BC
North East Baptist Temple
Old Way BC
Peace BC
Peace Temple BC
Philippian Full Gospel BC
Pilgrim BC
Pilgrim Land BC
Pilgrim Rest BC
Pleasant Grove BC
Progressive BC
Purity BC
Randall Memorial BC
Riggs Park BC
Saint Phillip BC
Second New St. Paul BC
Sharon BC
Southeast Baptist Tabernacle
St. James BC
St. John Freewill BC
St. Johns Primitive BC
St. Judah Spiritual BC
St. Paul BC
Tabernacle BC
Trinidad BC
Trinity BC
Unity BC
Upper Room BC
Zion BC of Eastland Gardens

| | | |
|---|---|---|
| Christian Methodist Episcopal (CME) (2) | - | Bunton Institutional CME Church |
| | | Lane Memorial CME Church |
| | | |
| Church Of God In Christ (COGIC) (5) | - | Kirkland Memorial COGIC |
| | | Master's Child Glorious COGIC |
| | | Rehoboth COGIC |
| | | St. Paul Temple COGIC |
| | | Zion Temple COGIC |
| | | |
| Holiness (19) | - | Bethel Church of God Holiness |
| | | Bethel Commandment Church |
| | | Emanuel Assembly Church of PAW |
| | | Faith United Church of Christ |
| | | First Church of Christ Holiness USA |
| | | Gate of Heaven Holy Church |
| | | Helping Hand Holy Church |
| | | Holy Land Spiritual Temple |
| | | Interdenominational Church of Lord Jesus |
| | | Love of Christ Church |
| | | Macedonia Holy Church on the Rock |
| | | Mt. Calvary Holy Church of Deliverance |
| | | New Hope FBH Church of God |
| | | Righteous Church of God |
| | | Righteous Church of God |
| | | Samuel Church of Christ |
| | | Tried Stone FBH Church |
| | | True Holiness Church of Christ |
| | | Zion Fair First Born Church of God |
| | | |
| Nondenominational (10) | - | Bethel New Light Gospel Church |
| | | Faith Bible Church |
| | | Faith Outreach Temple |
| | | Full Gospel Tabernacle Church |
| | | Macedonia Community Church |

| | |
|---|---|
| Nondenominational (Continued) | Miracle Temple of Faith<br>Mission Assembly of Jesus Christ<br>Rhema Christian Center<br>Right Way Christian Community Church<br>Scriptural Tabernacle |
| Pentecostal (6) | - Apostolic Evangelical Church<br>Apostolic Faith Church<br>Christian Faith Pentecostal Church<br>Church of Deliverance<br>Morningstar Pentecostal Church<br>Mt. Ephriam Pentecostal Church |
| Pentecostal/Holiness (0) | - None |
| United Church of Christ (0) | - None |
| UM (United Methodist) (8) | - Community UM Church<br>Douglas Memorial UM Church<br>Franklin B. Nash UM Church<br>Hughes Memorial UM Church<br>Lincoln Park UM Church<br>McKendree UM Church<br>Mt. Vernon UM Church<br>Randall Memorial UM Church |

# WASHINGTON, D.C. NORTHWEST SECTION - 170 churches

| | |
|---|---|
| African Methodist Episcopal (AME) (6) | - Galbraith AME Zion Church<br>Hemingway Temple AME Church<br>John Wesley AME Zion Church |

## Figure 13
## Denominational Percent of N.W. Churches

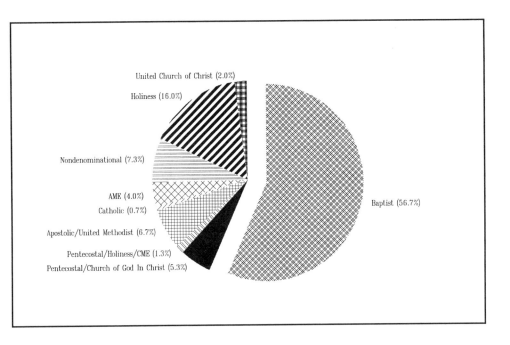

African Methodist Episcopal (Continued)

Metropolitan AME Church
St. Paul AME Zion Church
Trinity AME Zion Church

Apostolic (10)

- Bibleway Church
Christ Apostolic Church
First United Church of Jesus Christ

Apostolic (Continued)

Fisherman of Men Church
Friendship Church of Our Lord Jesus Christ
Little Temple Church
Mount Calvary Way of the Cross
Old Pentecost Church
Scripture Church
Washington Apostolic Church

Baptist (85)

- Abundant Life BC
Alexander Memorial BC
Berean BC
Bright Light BC
Calvary BC
Canaan BC
Carolina Missionary BC
Corinthian BC
Eternal Faith BC
Exodus Missionary BC
First BC
First Genesis BC
First Rising Mount Zion BC
Florida Avenue BC
Foundation BC
Freedom BC
Gethsemane BC
Gideon BC
Good News BC
Goodwill BC
Greater First Baptist-Mt. Pleasant
Greater Little Ark BC
Greater New Hope BC
Greater St. Paul BC
Iconium BC
Jerusalem BC

Baptist (Continued)

King Emmanuel BC
Lilly Memorial BC
Meridian Hill BC
Metropolitan BC
Morning Star BC
Mount Gideon BC
Mount Pleasant BC
Mt. Bethel BC
Mt. Calvary Free Will BC
Mt. Carmel BC
Mt. Gilead BC
Mt. Rona Missionary BC
Mt. Sinai BC
Mt. Zion BC
National Baptist Memorial Church
Nazareth BC
New Bethany BC
New Bethel BC
New Birth BC
New Fountain BC
New Home BC
New Mount Carmel BC
New Redeemer BC
New Second Baptist Mission Church
New Southern Rock BC
New Temple BC
Nineteenth Street BC
Northwest BC
Pentecost BC
Plain Truth BC
Redeemer BC
Refuge BC
Rising Sun BC
Rock Creek BC

Baptist (Continued)

Saint Marks BC
Salem BC
Second BC
Seventh Day BC
Shiloh BC
Sixteenth Street BC, Inc.
Southern BC
Southern Bethany BC
Springfield BC
St. Charles BC
St. John United BC
St. Joseph BC
St. Luke BC
St. Mary's BC
St. Stephen's BC
Temple BC
Tenth Street BC
Third BC
True Gospel BC
Verdadera Fe BC
Vermont Avenue BC
Victory Memorial BC
Walker Memorial BC
Zion BC
Zion Hill BC

Christian Methodist Episcopal (CME) (2)    -   Israel Metropolitan CME Church
                                               Miles Memorial CME Church

Church Of God In Christ (COGIC) (8)        -   Friendship COGIC
                                               Loye Temple COGIC
                                               Macedonia COGIC
                                               Morning Star COGIC
                                               New Bethel COGIC

Church Of God In Christ (Continued)

Star of Bethlehem COGIC
Star of Hope COGIC
Temple COGIC

Disciples of Christ (3)

- First Congregational Church
Lincoln Temple United Church of Christ
People's Congregational United Church

Holiness (24)

- Bethlehem Faith Bible Holiness Church
Christ Church
Christ Holy Tabernacle
Christian Holiness Pentecostal Church
Christian Tabernacle of God
Faithful Gospel Church of God
Garden of Prayer United Holiness Church
Grace Reformed Church
Highway Christian Church of Christ
Holy Commandment Church of God
Holy Tabernacle of Jesus Christ
International House of Prayer
Mount Olive Church of Christ
National Memorial Church of God
Newborn Church of God & True Holiness
Shepherd Park Community Church of God
Soul Saving Center Church of God
The Church of God
The New Testament Church in Jesus Christ
Third Street Church of God
True Grace Holy Temple Church of Christ
United Holiness Church of Deliverance
United House of Prayer for All People
United True Love Gospel Mission

Nondenominational (11)

- Emanuel Faith Tabernacle

Nondenominational (Continued)

Faith Assembly of Christ
Faith and Hope Full Gospel Church
Good Shepherd Interdenominational
Heavenly Host New Second Mt. Calvary
Oliver Temple Church
Park Road Community Church
Patterson Memorial Church
St. Mathews Overcoming Church of God
Third World and Peace Black Church
Upperway Church

Pentecostal (8)

- Church of the Living God Pillar
Ethiopian Community Evangelical Church
Free Evangelistic Church
Greater Mt. Calvary Holy Church
Michael's Temple Pentecostal Church
Mt. Joy Pentecostal SSS Church
Mt. Zion Pentecostal Church
Seventh Day Pentecostal Church

Pentecostal/Holiness (2)

- All Souls House of Prayer
Christian Home Pentecostal Holiness

United Methodist (UM) (10)

- Albright Memorial UM Church
Asbury UM Church
Brightwood Park UM Church
Dumbarton UM Church
Emory UM Church
Foundry UM Church
Metropolitan Memorial UM Church
Petworth UM Church
Simpson-Hamline UM Church
Van Buren UM Church

## Figure 14
## Denominational Percent of S.E. Churches

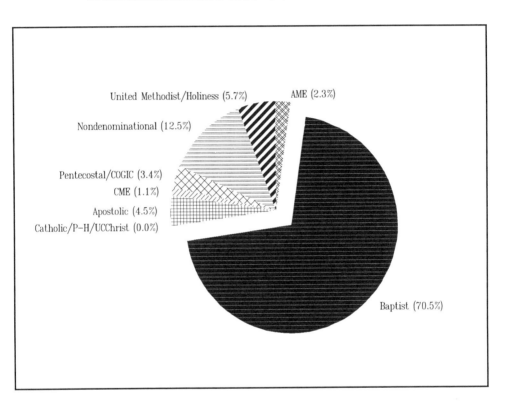

**WASHINGTON, D.C. SOUTHEAST SECTION - 96 churches**
African Methodist Episcopal (AME) (2)     -   Campbell AME Church

African Methodist Episcopal (Continued)       St. Lucille AME Zion Church

Apostolic (4)                          -  Apostolic Faith Church
                                          Bethuel Temple Church of Christ
                                          Grace Apostolic Church
                                          Shiloh Apostolic Church

Baptist (62)                           -  Ambassador BC
                                          Central BC
                                          Covenant BC
                                          Delaware Avenue BC
                                          East Washington Heights BC
                                          Edgewood BC
                                          Emanuel BC
                                          Faith BC
                                          First BC
                                          First BC of Marshall Heights
                                          First National BC
                                          First Rock BC
                                          First Rock BC
                                          Four Gospel BC
                                          Galilee BC
                                          Good Samaritan BC
                                          Grace Memorial BC
                                          Greater People Union BC
                                          Guiding Light Refuge BC
                                          Harvey Memorial BC
                                          Israel Memorial BC
                                          Johenning BC
                                          Johnson Memorial BC
                                          Liberty BC
                                          Macedonia BC
                                          Matthews Memorial BC
                                          Mentrotone BC

Baptist (Continued)

Mount Calvary BC
Mount Carmel Freewill BC
Mount Enon Missionary BC
Mount Ephraim BC
Mount Joy BC
Mt. Calvary BC
Mt. Moriah BC
Mt. Paran BC
New Hope Freewill BC
New Image Community BC
New Jerusalem Missionary BC
New Macedonia BC
New Morning Star BC
New United BC
Open Door BC
Paramount BC
Pennsylvania Avenue BC
Potomac BC
Providence BC
Rehoboth BC
Resurrection BC
Revelation BC
Second St. James BC
Sour Gospel BC
Southern Friendship BC
St. Matthew's BC
Temple Missionary BC
Thankful BC
Thomas Johns Memorial BC
True Gospel Tabernacle BC
True Way BC
Union Temple BC
Uplift BC
Vineyard BC

Baptist (Continued)            Word of God BC

Christian Methodist Episcopal (CME) (1)     -    St. John CME Church

Church Of God In Christ (COGIC) (3)     -    East Capitol COGIC
Greater Deliverance COGIC
Jesus Apostolic COGIC

Disciples of Christ (0)     -    None

Holiness (5)     -    Evening Light Church of Christ
Nationwide Unity Holy Church of God
Tried Stone Church of Christ
Universal Holiness Church
Young's Memorial Church of Christ

Nondenominational (11)     -    Anacostia Bible Church
Calvary Christian Church
Guiding Light Full Gospel Church
I Am Church of God, Inc.
Independent Church of God
Jesus Christ of Power Church
Mt. Calvary Evangelistic Church
Open Door Ministry
People's Church
Prayer Temple Church
Unity of Love Praise Temple

Pentecostal (3)     -    Church of Jesus Christ
Church of The Holy Trinity
Faith Tabernacle of Prayer

Pentecostal/Holiness (0)     -    None

United Methodist (UM) (5)

- A.P. Shaw UM Church
  Capitol Hill UM Church
  Ebenezer UM Church
  Jones Memorial UM Church
  Ryland Epworth UM Church

# Figure 15
# Denominational Percent of S.W. Churches

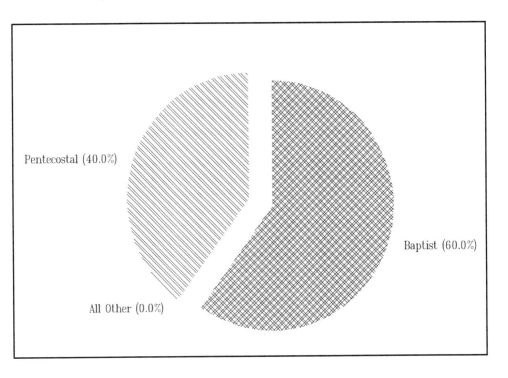

## WASHINGTON, D.C. SOUTHWEST SECTION - 5 churches

| | | |
|---|---|---|
| African Methodist Episcopal (AME) (0) | - | None |
| Apostolic (0) | - | None |
| Baptist (3) | - | Carron BC |
| | | Friendship BC |
| | | Riverside BC |
| Christian Methodist Episcopal (CME) (0) | - | None |
| Church Of God In Christ (COGIC) (0) | - | None |
| Disciples of Christ (0) | - | None |
| Holiness (0) | - | None |
| Nondenominational (0) | - | None |
| Pentecostal (2) | - | Bethel Pentecostal Tabernacle of the Assemblies of God |
| | | Redeemed Temple of Jesus Christ |
| Pentecostal/Holiness (0) | - | None |
| United Methodist (UM) (0) | - | None |

# *MARYLAND*
# *CHURCH DENOMINATIONAL LISTING*

Maryland has 133 Black churches. The ratio of churches per denomination for the state of Maryland is detailed in Figure 16 on the next page.

The data provided in Figure 16 shows that the Baptist denomination has 30.8% of the churches. It is the leading form of religion in Maryland. The Pentecostal and Holiness denominations rank second and third respectfully, while Nondenominational churches are fourth.

African Methodist Episcopal churches are ranked fifth and the Church of God in Christ churches are sixth. The Apostolic churches are seventh and the United Methodist church rank eighth, while the Christian Methodist Episcopal churches rank ninth. The Disciples of Christ and Pentecostal/Holiness churches each have the same percentages and are ranked tenth.

### Table 8 - Number of Churches Per Denomination in Maryland

| | |
|---|---|
| African Methodist Episcopal (AME) | ( 9) |
| Apostolic | ( 5) |
| Baptist | (41) |
| Christian Methodist Episcopal (CME) | ( 1) |
| Church of God In Christ (COGIC) | ( 8) |
| Disciples of Christ | ( 0) |
| Holiness | (21) |
| Nondenominational | (20) |
| Pentecostal | (26) |
| Pentecostal/Holiness | ( 0) |
| United Methodist (UM) | ( 2) |

## Figure 16
## Denominational Percent of Maryland Churches

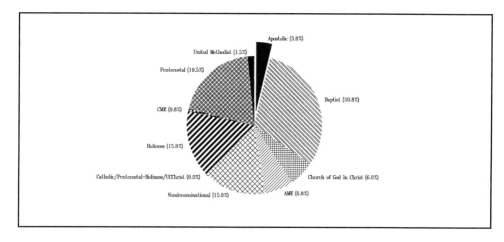

## MARYLAND CHURCHES

| | |
|---|---|
| African Methodist Episcopal (AME) (9) | - Clinton AME Zion Church |
| | Ebenezer AME Church |
| | Full Gospel AME Zion Church |
| | Greater Mt. Nebo AME Zion Church |
| | Hemingway Memorial AME Church |
| | Hunter Memorial AME Church |
| | Mt. Pisgah AME Church |
| | Scotland AME Zion Church |
| | Seaton Memorial AME Church |
| | |
| Apostolic (5) | - Assembly Church of our Lord Jesus |
| | Calvary Apostolic Church |
| | Christ Temple Church-Apostolic Faith |
| | National Apostolic Church |
| | Zion Church of Jesus Christ Apostolic |
| | |
| Baptist (41) | - Abssyinia BC |
| | Ascension BC |
| | Bible BC of D.C. |
| | Carmody Hills BC |
| | Decatur Heights BC |
| | Fellowship BC of Boulevard Heights |
| | First BC of District Heights |
| | First BC-Fairmont Heights |
| | First BC of Glenarden |
| | First BC of Guilford |
| | First BC of Highland Park |
| | First BC of Hyattsville |
| | First New Horizon BC |
| | Freedom Way BC |
| | Haitian Baptist Mission |
| | Jordan BC |
| | Macedonia BC |

Baptist (Continued)

Maple Springs BC
Mt. Ararat BC
Mt. Ennon BC
New Haven BC
New Hope BC
New Life Full Gospel BC
Parker Memorial BC
Parkview BC
Parkway BC
Peaceful Bible BC
Refuge BC
Revelation BC
Round Oak BC
Seat Pleasant BC
Shiloh BC
Shining Star BC
Spirit of Peace BC
Spirit of Peace BC
Spirit of Peace BC
Spirit of Peace BC
St. Paul BC
St. John Baptist De LaSalle
Sylvan Vista BC
Zion BC

Christian Methodist Episcopal (CME) (1)    -    Capitol Heights CME Church

Church Of God In Christ (COGIC) (8)    -    Garden of Gethsemane COGIC
Glenarden COGIC
Grace Temple COGIC
Living Word COGIC
Newborn COGIC
Refreshing Springs COGIC
Ridgely COGIC

171

Church of God in Christ (Continued)        Temple COGIC

Disciples of Christ (0)         -  None

Holiness (21)         -  Christian Tabernacle Holy Church
           Faithful Holiness Church
           Holy Trinity-Denomination House of Prayer
           Independent Church of Christ
           Interdenominational Church of Christ
           Lighthouse Church
           Lighthouse Church
           Lighthouse Full Gospel Mission Church
           Little Child Holy Church On The Rock
           Love Temple Church of Deliverance
           New St. James United Holy Church
           One Way United Holiness Church
           Refuge Church of Christ
           Righteous Church of Holiness Inc.
           Straight Way Church of Christ
           True Deliverance Church of God
           United Fellowship Church
           United Holiness Deliverance Church
           Wayside Holiness Church Assembly of God
           Way of Life Church of Christ
           Youth for Christ Mission

Nondenominational (20)       -  Christian Hope Center
           Community Temple Church
           Craig Memorial Community Church
           Freedom Church
           Harvest Church International, Inc.
           Interdenominational Church of God
           Metro World Outreach Center
           Mt. Airy Full Gospel Church

Nondenominational (Continued)

New Covenant Church
New Testament Church
Outreach Christian Center
Overcomers Gospel Church
Redeeming Love Christian Center
Sacred Hour Full Gospel
Sermon on the Mount
Shekinah Worship Center
Solid Rock Church
Tree of Life Fellowship
Victory Temple
Word Christian Center

Pentecostal (26)

- Apostolic United Pentecostal Church
Christ Mission Church
Christ Outreach Temple
Christian Deliverance Fellowship
Church of Deliverance
Church of God of Prophecy
Church of God of Silver Spring
College Park Pentecostal Holiness Church
Crusader's Youth Revival Church
Deliverance Church of Christ
Deliverance Temple Christian Church
Divine Mission Faith Bible Church
East Side Holy Trinity Church, Inc.
Emmanuel Assembly
Emmanuel Grace Tabernacle, Inc.
Faith Pentecostal Holiness Church
Faith Temple Number Two
Fidelity Christian Center
First United Church-Fairmont Heights
First United Pentecostal Church
Free Gospel Church of Christ, Inc.

| | |
|---|---|
| Pentecostal (Continued) | Friendship AOH Church of God |
| | Greater Church of Deliverance |
| | International Church of Christ Ministry |
| | Pentecostal Evangelical Church |
| | Pentecostal Holiness Church |
| Pentecostal/Holiness (0) | - None |
| United Methodist (UM) (2) | - Gethsemane UM Church |
| | Grace UM Church |

# *VIRGINIA*
## *CHURCH DENOMINATIONAL LISTING*

Virginia has 42 Black churches. The ratio of churches per denomination for the state of Virginia is detailed in Figure 17 on the next page.

The data provided in Figure 17 shows that the Baptist denomination has 35.9% of the churches. It is the leading form of religion in Virginia. The Pentecostal churches are ranked second. The United Methodist churches are third, while the Holiness churches are fourth.

Nondenominational churches rank fifth and the Apostolic and Christian Methodist Episcopal churches are sixth. The Church of God in Christ and the Christian Methodist Episcopal churches have the same percentages each and rank seventh respectfully. The Disciples of Christ and Pentecostal/Holiness churches also have the same percentages and are ranked ninth.

### Table 9 - Number of Churches Per Denomination in Virginia

| | |
|---|---|
| African Methodist Episcopal (AME) | ( 1) |
| Apostolic | ( 2) |
| Baptist | ( 14) |
| Christian Methodist Episcopal (CME) | ( 2) |
| Church of God In Christ (COGIC) | ( 1) |
| Disciples of Christ | ( 0) |
| Holiness | ( 5) |
| Nondenominational | ( 3) |
| Pentecostal | ( 8) |
| Pentecostal/Holiness | ( 0) |
| United Methodist (UM) | ( 6) |

## Figure 17
## Denominational Percent of Virginia Churches

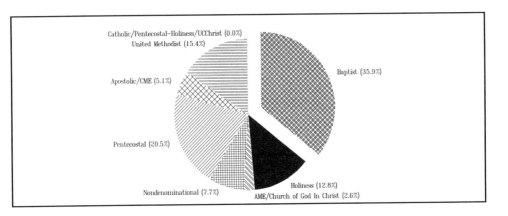

# VIRGINIA CHURCHES

| | | |
|---|---|---|
| African Methodist Episcopal (AME) (1) | - | Lomax AME Zion Church |
| Apostolic (2) | - | Bibleway Church of our Lord Jesus<br>New Apostolic Church |
| Baptist (14) | - | Alfred Street BC<br>Baptist Temple Baptist<br>Bethlehem BC<br>Beulah BC<br>Crossroads BC<br>Ebenezer BC<br>Ebenezer BC<br>Macedonia BC<br>Mount Olive BC<br>Mount Pleasant BC<br>Mount Salvation BC<br>Shiloh BC<br>Third BC<br>Warner BC |
| Christian Methodist Episcopal (CME) (2) | - | Mead Memorial Episcopal Church<br>Russell Temple CME Church |
| Church Of God In Christ (COGIC) (1) | - | Gethsemane COGIC |
| Disciples of Christ (0) | - | None |
| Holiness (5) | - | Abundant Life United Holy Church<br>Antioch Church of Christ<br>Golden Church of God of Prophecy |

Holiness (Continued)

Mount Calvary Holy Church of America
St. Paul Pentecostal United Holy Church

Nondenominational (3)

- New Life Open Bible Church
Ship of Zion Church
Spirit of Faith Ministries

Pentecostal (8)

- Bridal Call of Christ Church
Church of God of Prophecy
Love of Christ Church
Mount Ne-Bo Pentecostal Church
St. Paul Pentecostal Church
United Faith Pentecostal Church
United Pentecostal Church
United Pentecostal Church of Herndon

Pentecostal/Holiness (0)

- None

United Methodist (UM) (6)

- Aldersgate UM Church
Asbury UM Church
Galloway UM Church
Mount Olivet UM Church
Roberts Memorial UM Church
Woodlawn UM Church

# *PART II*
# *WASHINGTON, D.C., MARYLAND AND VIRGINIA CHURCH LISTING*

This section provides a detailed listing of the black churches in Washington, D.C., Maryland and Virginia. Addresses and zip codes are listed for all churches in the aforementioned areas.

## WASHINGTON, D.C. CHURCHES

## CHURCHES - NORTHEAST

Antioch Baptist Church
1105 50th Street, N.E.
Washington, D.C. 20019

Apostolic Evangelical Church
 of Jesus Christ
34 14th Street, N.E.
Washington, D.C. 20002

Apostolic Faith Church
513 M Street, N.E.
Washington, D.C. 20002

Beth Shalom AME Zion Church
1249 Bladensburg Road, N.E.
Washington, D.C. 20002

Bethel Commandment Church
1627 Kenilworth Avenue, N.E.
Washington, D.C. 20019

Bethel New Light Gospel Church
331 15th Street, N.E.
Washington, D.C. 20002

Bethesda Baptist Church
1808 Capitol Avenue, N.E.
Washington, D.C. 20002

Bethlehem Church of God Holiness
5898 Eastern Avenue, N.E.
Washington, D.C. 20011

Beulah Baptist Church of
 Deanwood Heights
5820 Dix Street, N.E.
Washington, D.C. 20019

Bible Baptist Church
4421 Jay Street, N.E.
Washington, D.C. 20019

Brookland Union Baptist Church
3101 14th Street, N.E.
Washington, D.C. 20017

Brown Memorial AME Church
130 14th Street, N.E.
Washington, D.C. 20002

Bunton Institutional CME Church
1350 Lawrence Street, N.E.
Washington, D.C. 20017

Central Union Baptist Church
4401 Foote Street, N.E.
Washington, D.C. 20019

Charity Baptist Church
600 9th Street, N.E.
Washington, D.C. 20002

Christian Faith Pentecostal Church
216 K Street, N.E.
Washington, D.C. 20002

Christian Love Baptist Church
818 Bladensburg Road, N.E.
Washington, D.C. 20002

Church of Deliverance
1201 I Street, N.E.
Washington, D.C. 20002

Church of the Lord Jesus Christ
of the Apostolic Faith
1230 C Street, N.E.
Washington, D.C. 20002

Community UM Church
1600 Levis Street, N.E.
Washington, D.C. 20002

Contee Mae Zion Church
903 Division Avenue, N.E.
Washington, D.C. 20019

Daughter of Zion Baptist Church
2964 Mills Avenue, N.E.
Washington, D.C. 20018

Deutoronomy Missionary Baptist
1007 H Street, N.E.
Washington, D.C. 20002

Divine Love Baptist Church
4303 Sheriff Road, N.E.
Washington, D.C. 20019

Douglas Memorial UM Church
11th & H Streets, N.E.
Washington, D.C. 20002

East Friendship Baptist Church
4401 Brooks Street, N.E.
Washington, D.C. 20019

Ebenezer Baptist Church
44 Q Street, N.E.
Washington, D.C. 20001

Emanuel Assembly Church of the
Pentecostal Assemblies of the World
1327 Constitution Avenue, N.E.
Washington, D.C. 20002

Enon Baptist Church
505 L Street, N.E.
Washington D.C. 20002

Evergreen Baptist Church
5001 Grant Street, N.E.
Washington, D.C. 20019

Faith Bible Church
1350 Maryland Avenue, N.E.
Washington, D.C. 20002

Faith Outreach Temple
310 62nd Street, N.E.
Washington, D.C. 20019

Faith United Church of Christ
4900 10th Street, N.E.
Washington, D.C. 20017

Fellowship Baptist Church
1100 Bladensburg Road, N.E.
Washington, D.C. 20002

First Baptist Church of Deanwood
1008 45th Street, N.E.
Washington, D.C. 20019

First Church of Christ Holiness USA
1219 Hamlin Street, N.E.
Washington, D.C. 20017

Franklin B. Nash United
  Methodist Church
2001 Lincoln Road, N.E.
Washington, D.C. 20002

First Jericho Baptist Church
304 S Street, N.E.
Washington, D.C. 20002

First New Hope Baptist Church
1822 Third Street, N.E.
Washington, D.C. 20002

Full Gospel Tabernacle Church
632 11th Street, N.E.
Washington, D.C. 20002

Greater Friendly Baptist Church
404 13th Street, N.E.
Washington, D.C. 20002

Galatians Baptist Church
806 F Street, N.E.
Washington, D.C. 20002

Gate of Heaven Holy Church
2932 12th Street, N.E.
Washington, D.C. 20017

Glendale Baptist Church
4504 Gault Place, N.E.
Washington, D.C. 20019

Grace Temple Bibleway Church
2901 12th Street, N.E.
Washington, D.C. 20017

Greater Mount Zion Baptist Church
609 Maryland Avenue, N.E.
Washington, D.C. 20002

Greater Mt. Pisgah Baptist Church
1818 Gales Street, N.E.
Washington, D.C. 20002

Greater Pleasant Grove Baptist Church
1101 4th Street, N.E.
Washington, D.C. 20002

Greater Victory Baptist Church
2100 4th Street, N.E.
Washington, D.C. 20002

Guiding Star Baptist Church
1025 Jackson Street, N.E.
Washington, D.C. 20017

Guildfield Baptist Church
1023 Otis Street, N.E.
Washington, D.C. 20017

Helping Hand Holy Church, Inc.
2323 First Street, N.E.
Washington, D.C. 20001

Holy Land Spiritual Temple
1120 Montello Avenue, N.E.
Washington, D.C. 20002

Holy Trinity Missionary Baptist Church
1244 Florida Avenue, N.E.
Washington, D.C. 20009

Holyway Baptist Church
516 H Street, N.E.
Washington, D.C. 20002

Hughes Memorial UM Church
53rd & Ames Street, N.E.
Washington, D.C. 20019

Interdenominational Church of
 Lord Jesus
716 15th Street, N.E.
Washington, D.C. 20002

Isle of Patmos Baptist Church
12th and Rhode Island Avenue, N.E.
Washington, D.C. 20005

Israel Baptist Church
1251 Saratoga Avenue, N.E.
Washington, D.C. 20002

James Memorial Baptist Church
1723 Third Street, N.E.
Washington, D.C. 20002

Jericho Baptist Church
4419 Douglas Street, N.E.
Washington, D.C. 20019

Kingdom of Zion Baptist Church
1037 Bladensburg Road, N.E.
Washington, D.C. 20002

Kirkland Memorial COGIC
624 8th Street, N.E.
Washington, D.C. 20002

Lane Memorial CME Church
1423 C Street, N.E.
Washington, D.C. 20002

Lincoln Park UM Church
1301 N.C. Avenue, N.E.
Washington, D.C. 20019

Love of Christ Church
431 15th Street, N.E.
Washington, D.C. 20002

Macedonia Community Church
1026 46th Street, N.E.
Washington, D.C. 20019

Macedonia Holy Church on the Rock
707 Division Avenue, N.E.
Washington, D.C. 20020

Master's Child Glorious Church
 of God In Christ
2715 22nd Street, N.E.
Washington, D.C. 20002

McKendree UM Church
3321 24th Street, N.E.
Washington, D.C. 20018

Miracle Temple of Faith
1012 H Street, N.E.
Washington, D.C. 20002

Miracle from God Apostolic Church
3906 12th Street, N.E.
Washington, D.C. 20017

Mission Assembly of Jesus Christ
400 13th Street, N.E.
Washington, D.C. 20002

Morningstar Pentecostal Church
4417 Dix Street, N.E.
Washington, D.C. 20019

Mount Jezrell Baptist Church
405 Riggs Road, N.E.
Washington, D.C. 20011

Mount Siloam Baptist Church
342 8th Street, N.E.
Washington, D.C. 20004

Mt. Airy Baptist Church
1100 North Capitol Street, N.E.
Washington, D.C. 20002

Mt. Calvary Holy Church of
  Deliverance
5900 New Hampshire Avenue, N.E.
Washington, D.C. 20011

Mt. Ephriam Pentecostal Church
2200 4th Street, N.E.
Washington, D.C. 20002

Mt. Horeb Baptist Church
2914 Bladensburg Road, N.E.
Washington, D.C. 20018

Mt. Olive Baptist Church
1140 Sixth Street, N.E.
Washington, D.C. 20002

Mt. Vernon UM Church
1910 West Virginia Avenue, N.E.
Washington, D.C. 20002

New Birth Missionary Baptist Church
4918 Nannie Helen Burroughs N.E.
Washington, D.C. 20019

New Birth Prayer Missionary
  Baptist Church
4515 Sheriff Road, N.E.
Washington, D.C. 20019

New Canaan Baptist Church
701 15th Street, N.E.
Washington, D.C. 20002

New Covenant Baptist Church
4410 Hunt Place, N.E.
Washington, D.C. 20019

New Genesis Baptist Church
3501 12th Street, N.E.
Washington, D.C. 20017

New Hope FBH Church of God
811 48th Street, N.E.
Washington, D.C. 20019

New Horizon Baptist Church
217 16th Street, N.E.
Washington, D.C. 20002

New Life Baptist Church
1501 West Virginia Avenue, N.E.
Washington, D.C. 20002

New Light Missionary Baptist Church
3518 18th Street, N.E.
Washington, D.C. 20002

New Mount Calvary Baptist Church
4318 Sheriff Road, N.E.
Washington, D.C. 20019

New Mount Olive Baptist Church
710 58th Street, N.E.
Washington, D.C. 20019

New Samaritan Baptist Church
1100 Florida Avenue, N.E.
Washington, D.C. 20009

New St. John Missionary Baptist Church
2432 4th Street, N.E.
Washington, D.C. 20002

North East Baptist Temple
5325 East Capitol Street, N.E.
Washington, D.C. 20020

Old Way Baptist Church
1366 H Street, N.E.
Washington, D.C. 20002

Peace Baptist Church
712 18th Street, N.E.
Washington, D.C. 20002

Peace Temple Baptist Church
1138 Sixth Street, N.E.
Washington, D.C. 20002

Philippian Full Gospel Baptist
Church
5341 Jay Street, N.E.
Washington, D.C. 20019

Pilgrim AME Church
606 17th Street, N.E.
Washington, D.C. 20002

Pilgrim Baptist Church
700 I Street, N.E.
Washington, D.C. 20002

Pilgrim Land Baptist Church
5119 Nannie Helen Burghs. Ave., N.E.
Washington, D.C. 20019

Pilgrim Rest Baptist Church
4601 Sheriff Road, N.E.
Washington, D.C. 20019

Pleasant Grove Baptist Church
1800 Hamlin Street, N.E.
Washington, D.C. 20018

Progressive Baptist Church
1201 F Street, N.E.
Washington, D.C. 20002

Purity Baptist Church
1325 Maryland Avenue, N.E.
Washington, D.C. 20002

Randall Memorial Baptist Church
3200 22nd Street, N.E.
Washington, D.C. 20018

Randall Memorial UM Church
1002 46th Street, N.E.
Washington, D.C. 20019

Rehoboth Church of God In Christ
4242 Benning Road, N.E.
Washington, D.C. 20019

Reid Temple AME Church
1335 Michigan Avenue, N.E.
Washington, D.C.

Rhema Christian Center
4915 Sargent Road, N.E.
Washington, D.C. 20017

Riggs Park Baptist Church
5998 Chillum Place, N.E.
Washington, D.C. 20011

Right Way Christian Community Church
2009 Kearny Street, N.E.
Washington, D.C. 20018

Righteous Church of God
616 56th Street, N.E.
Washington, D.C. 20019

Saint Phillip Baptist Church
1001 North Capitol Street, N.E.
Washington, D.C. 20002

Samuel Church of Christ
403 H Street, N.E.
Washington, D.C. 20002

Second New St. Paul Baptist Church
2400 Franklin Street, N.E.
Washington, D.C. 20018

Sharon Baptist Church
3825 26th Street, N.E.
Washington, D.C. 20018

Southeast Baptist Tabernacle
4101 First Street, N.E.
Washington, D.C. 20011

Spiritual Tabernacle
337 K Street, N.E.
Washington, D.C. 20002

St. Benedict the Moor Center
320 21st Street, N.E.
Washington, D.C. 20002

St. James Baptist Church
4024 Minnesota Avenue, N.E.
Washington, D.C. 20019

St. John Freewill Baptist Church
4270 Benning Road, N.E.
Washington, D.C. 20019

St. Johns Primitive Baptist Church
1015 D Street, N.E.
Washington, D.C. 20002

186

St. Judah Spiritual Baptist Church
43 Anacostia Road, N.E.
Washington, D.C. 20019

St. Paul Baptist Church
1611 Brentwood Road, N.E.
Washington, D.C. 20018

St. Paul Temple COGIC
3420 16th Street, N.E.
Washington, D.C. 20018

Straitegate Bibleway Church
523 8th Street, N.E.
Washington, D.C. 20002

Tabernacle Baptist Church
719 Division Avenue, N.E.
Washington, D.C. 20019

The Whole Truth Church of the
 Lord Jesus Christ
2800 Douglas Street, N.E.
Washington, D.C. 20018

Tried Stone FBH Church
256 13th Street, N.E.
Washington, D.C. 20002

Trinidad Baptist Church
1611 Benning Road, N.E.
Washington, D.C. 20020

Trinity Baptist Church
1814 Central Place, N.E.
Washington, D.C. 20002

True Holiness Church of Christ
5821 East Capitol Street, N.E.
Washington, D.C. 20019

Union Wesley AME Zion Church
1860 Michigan Avenue, N.E.
Washington, D.C. 20018

Unity Baptist Church
424 Third Street, N.E.
Washington, D.C. 20002

Upper Room Baptist Church
60 Burns Street, N.E.
Washington, D.C. 20019

Varick Memorial AME Zion Church
255 Anacostia Avenue, N.E.
Washington, D.C. 20019

Ward Memorial AME Church
241 42nd Street, N.E.
Washington, D.C. 20019

Way of the Cross Church of Christ
332 9th Street, N.E.
Washington, D.C. 20002

Zion Baptist of Eastland Gardens
1234 Kenilworth Avenue, N.E.
Washington, D.C. 20019

Zion Fair First Born Church of
 the Living God
721 48th Street, N.E.
Washington, D.C. 20019

Zion Temple Church of God In Christ
1910 4th Street, N.E.
Washington, D.C. 20002


## CHURCHES - NORTHWEST


Abundant Life Baptist Church
1627 New Jersey Avenue, N.W.
Washington, D.C. 20001

Alexander Memorial Baptist Church
2709 N Street, N.W.
Washington, D.C. 20007

All Souls House of Prayer
1800 6th Street, N.W.
Washington, D.C. 20001

Albright Memorial UM Church
411 Rittenhouse Street, N.W.
Washington, D.C. 20011

Asbury United Methodist Church
926 11th Street, N.W.
Washington, D.C. 20001

Augustine Catholic Church
1425 V Street, N.W.
Washington, D.C. 20009

Berean Baptist Church
924 Madison Street, N.W.
Washington, D.C. 20011

Bethlehem Faith Bible Holiness Church
1532 North Capitol Street, N.W.
Washington, D.C. 20011

Bibleway Church
1130 New Jersey Avenue, N.W.
Washington, D.C. 20001

Bright Light Baptist Church
3231 Sherman Avenue, N.W.
Washington, D.C. 20010

Brightwood Park UM Church
8th and Jefferson Street, N.W.
Washington, D.C. 20010

Calvary Baptist Church
755 8th Street, N.W.
Washington, D.C. 20001

Canaan Baptist Church
1607 Monroe Street, N.W.
Washington, D.C. 20010

Carolina Missionary Baptist Church
777 Morton Street, N.W.
Washington, D.C. 20010

Christ Church
2855 Massachusetts Avenue, N.W.
Washington, D.C. 20008

Christ Apostolic Church
1545 6th Street, N.W.
Washington, D.C. 20001

Christ Holy Tabernacle
115 Rhode Island Avenue, N.W.
Washington, D.C. 20001

Christian Holiness Pentecostal Church
1700 10th Street, N.W.
Washington, D.C. 20001

Christian Home Pentecostal Holiness
  Church of God of America
1551 6th Street, N.W.
Washington, D.C. 20001

Christian Tabernacle of God
3707 Georgia Avenue, N.W.
Washington, D.C. 20010

Church of the Living God Pillar
1206 4th Street, N.W.
Washington, D.C. 20001

Corinthian Baptist Church
500 I Street, N.W.
Washington, D.C. 20001

Dumbarton UM Church
3133 Dumbarton Avenue, N.W.
Washington, D.C. 20007

Emanuel Faith Tabernacle
215 Upshur Street, N.W.
Washington, D.C.

Emory UM Church
6100 Georgia Avenue, N.W.
Washington, D.C. 20011

Eternal Faith Baptist Church
3714 14th Street, N.W.
Washington, D.C. 20010

Ethiopian Community Evangelical
  Church
1906 H Street, N.W.
Washington, D.C. 20006

Exodus Missionary Baptist Church
901 Rittenhouse, N.W.
Washington, D.C. 20011

Faith Assembly of Christ
4825 Georgia Avenue, N.W.
Washington, D.C. 20010

Faith and Hope Full Gospel Church
90 P Street, N.W.
Washington, D.C. 20001

Faithful Gospel Church of God
609 Kennedy Street, N.W.
Washington, D.C. 20011

First Baptist Church
712 Randolph Street, N.W.
Washington, D.C. 20011

First Congregational Church
10th & G Streets, N.W.
Washington, D.C. 20004

First Genesis Baptist Church
1527 12th Street, N.W.
Washington, D.C. 20005

First Rising Mount Zion Baptist Church
1240 Sixth Street, N.W.
Washington, D.C. 20001

First United Church of Jesus
  Christ Apostolic
7901 16th Street, N.W.
Washington, D.C. 20012

Fisherman of Men Church
3641 Georgia Avenue, N.W.
Washington, D.C. 20010

Florida Avenue Baptist Church
623 Florida Avenue, N.W.
Washington, D.C. 20001

Foundation Baptist Church
1707 14th Street, N.W.
Washington, D.C. 20009

Foundry UM Church
1500 16th Street, N.W.
Washington, D.C. 20036

Freedom Baptist Church
1519 U Street, N.W.
Washington, D.C. 20009

Free Evangelistic Church
1840 14th Street, N.W.
Washington, D.C. 20010

Friendship Church of God In Christ
3900 Kansas Avenue, N.W.
Washington, D.C. 20011

Friendship Church of Lord Jesus Christ
4001 14th Street, N.W.
Washington, D.C. 20011

Galbraith AME Zion Church
1114 6th Street, N.W.
Washington, D.C. 20001

Garden of Prayer United
  Holiness Church
6905 4th Street, N.W.
Washington, D.C. 20012

Gethsemane Baptist Church
5119 4th Street, N.W.
Washington, D.C. 20011

Good News Baptist Church
2301 Sherman Avenue, N.W.
Washington, D.C. 20001

Good Shepherd Interdenominational
1838 11th Street, N.W.
Washington, D.C. 20001

Goodwill Baptist Church
1862 Kalorama Road, N.W.
Washington, D.C. 20009

Grace Reformed Church
1405 15th Street, N.W.
Washington, D.C. 20005

Greater First Baptist-Mt. Pleasant
13th and Fairmont, N.W.
Washington, D.C. 20001

Greater Little Ark Baptist Church
150 S Street, N.W.
Washington, D.C. 20001

Greater Mt. Calvary Holy Church
625-627 Park Road, N.W.
Washington, D.C. 20010

Greater New Hope Baptist Church
816 8th Street, N.W.
Washington, D.C. 20001

Greater St. Paul Baptist Church
5720 South Dakota Avenue, N.W.
Washington, D.C. 20011

Heavenly Host New Second
 Mt. Calvary Church
827 Kennedy Street, N.W.
Washington, D.C. 20011

Hemingway Temple AME Church
501 P Street, N.W.
Washington, D.C. 20001

Highway Christian Church of Christ
432 W Street, N.W.
Washington, D.C.

Holy Commandment Church of God
3507 22nd Street, N.W.
Washington, D.C. 20008

Holy Tabernacle of Jesus Christ
4130 Georgia Avenue, N.W.
Washington, D.C. 20010

Iconium Baptist Church
4917 Georgia Avenue, N.W.
Washington, D.C. 20011

International House of Prayer
3700 Georgia Avenue, N.W.
Washington, D.C. 20010

Israel Metropolitan CME Church
557 Randolph Street, N.W.
Washington, D.C. 20011

Jerusalem Baptist Church
26th and P Street, N.W.
Washington, D.C. 20037

John Wesley AME Zion Church
1615 14th Street, N.W.
Washington, D.C. 20009

King Emmanuel Baptist Church
1725 Kalorama Road, N.W.
Washington, D.C. 20009

Lilly Memorial Baptist Church
460 K Street, N.W.
Washington, D.C. 20001

Lincoln Temple United Church
 of Christ
1701 11th Street, N.W.
Washington, D.C. 20001

Little Temple Church
3308 Georgia Avenue, N.W.
Washington, D.C. 20010

Loye Temple Church of God In Christ
3547 Georgia Avenue, N.W.
Washington, D.C. 20010

Macedonia Church of God In Christ
1320 Farragut Street, N.W.
Washington, D.C. 20011

Meridian Hill Baptist Church
3146 16th Street, N.W.
Washington, D.C. 20010

Metropolitan AME Church
1518 M Street, N.W.
Washington, D.C. 20005

Metropolitan Baptist Church
1225 R Street, N.W.
Washington, D.C. 20001

Metropolitan Memorial UM Church
3401 Nebraska Avenue, N.W.
Washington, D.C. 20016

Michael's Temple Pentecostal Church
5517 Colorado Avenue, N.W.
Washington, D.C.

Miles Memorial CME Church
501 N Street, N.W.
Washington, D.C. 20001

Morning Star Baptist Church
531 T Street, N.W.
Washington, D.C. 20001

Morning Star COGIC
443 Kennedy Street, N.W.
Washington, D.C. 20011

Mt. Calvary Free Will Baptist Church
4408-1/2 Georgia Avenue, N.W.
Washington, D.C. 20010

Mount Calvary Way of the Cross
  Church of Christ
129 Kennedy Street, N.W.
Washington, D.C. 20011

Mount Gideon Baptist Church
901 Ingraham Street, N.W.
Washington, D.C. 20011

Mount Olive Church of Christ
1418 New Jersey Avenue, N.W.
Washington, D.C. 20001

Mount Pleasant Baptist Church
215 Rhode Island Avenue, N.W.
Washington, D.C. 20001

Mt. Bethel Baptist Church
Mt and Rhode Island Ave., N.W.
Washington, D.C. 20001

Mt. Carmel Baptist Church
901 Third Street, N.W.
Washington, D.C. 20001

Mt. Gilead Baptist Church
1625 13th Street, N.W.
Washington, D.C. 20009

192

Mt. Joy Pentecostal SSS Church
432 M Street, N.W.
Washington, D.C. 20001

Mt. Rona Missionary Baptist Church
3431 13th Street, N.W.
Washington, D.C. 20010

Mt. Sinai Baptist Church
1615 Third Street, N.W.
Washington, D.C. 20001

Mt. Zion Baptist Church
5101 14th Street, N.W.
Washington, D.C. 20011

Mt. Zion Pentecostal Church
1112 N Street, N.W.
Washington, D.C. 20001

National Baptist Memorial Church
1501 Columbia Road, N.W.
Washington, D.C. 20009

National Memorial Church of God
4100 16th Street, N.W.
Washington, D.C. 20011

Nazareth Baptist Church
3935 7th Street, N.W.
Washington, D.C. 20011

New Bethany Baptist Church
1300 10th Street, N.W.
Washington, D.C. 20001

New Bethel Baptist Church
1739 9th Street, N.W.
Washington, D.C. 20001

New Bethel Church of God In Christ
6440 Piney Branch Road, N.W.
Washington, D.C. 20012

New Birth Baptist Church
1200 Kirby Street, N.W.
Washington, D.C. 20001

New Fountain Baptist Church
1210 Eighth Street, N.W.
Washington, D.C. 20001

New Home Baptist Church
3423 Holmead Place, N.W.
Washington, D.C. 20010

New Mount Carmel Baptist Church
4100 Illinois Avenue, N.W.
Washington, D.C. 20011

New Redeemer Baptist Church
5714 Georgia Avenue, N.W.
Washington, D.C. 20011

New Second Baptist Mission Church
7205 Georgia Avenue, N.W.
Washington, D.C. 20012

New Southern Rock Baptist Church
750 Buchannan Street, N.W.
Washington, D.C. 20011

New Temple Baptist Church
4208 7th Street, N.W.
Washington, D.C. 20011

Newborn Church of God & True
  Holiness Church
916 Rittenhouse, N.W.
Washington, D.C. 20011

Nineteenth Street Baptist Church
4606 16th Street, N.W.
Washington, D.C. 20011

Northwest Baptist Church
3226 Georgia Avenue, N.W.
Washington, D.C. 20010

Old Pentecost Church
727 Hobart Place, N.W.
Washington, D.C. 20001

Oliver Temple Church
3555 Georgia Avenue, N.W.
Washington, D.C. 20010

Park Road Community Church
1019 Park Road, N.W.
Washington, D.C. 20010

Patterson Memorial Church
642 Rock Creek Church Road, N.W.
Washington, D.C. 20010

Pentecost Baptist Church
2107 10th Street, N.W.
Washington, D.C. 20001

People's Congregational United
  Church of Christ
4704 13th Street, N.W.
Washington, D.C. 20011

Petworth UM Church
32 Grant Circle, N.W.
Washington, D.C. 20011

Plain Truth Baptist Church
304 Kennedy Street, N.W.
Washington, D.C. 20011

Redeemer Baptist Church
528 Kennedy Street, N.W.
Washington, D.C. 20011

Refuge Baptist Church
1851 Ninth Street, N.W.
Washington, D.C. 20001

Rising Sun Baptist Church
3702 13th Street, N.W.
Washington, D.C. 20010

Rock Creek Baptist Church
4201 Eighth Street, N.W.
Washington, D.C. 20011

Saint Marks Baptist Church
624 Underwood Street, N.W.
Washington, D.C. 20012

Salem Baptist Church
917 N Street, N.W.
Washington, D.C. 20001

Scripture Church
810 0 Street, N.W.
Washington, D.C. 20001

Second Baptist Church
816 Third Street, N.W.
Washington, D.C. 20001

Seventh Day Baptist Church
4700 16th Street, N.W.
Washington, D.C. 20011

Seventh Day Pentecostal Church
 of the Living God
1443 Euclid Street, N.W.
Washington, D.C.

Shepherd Park Community Church of God
7239 Georgia Avenue, N.W.
Washington, D.C. 20012

Shiloh Baptist Church
1500 9th Street, N.W.
Washington, D.C. 20001

Simpson-Hamline United Methodist
4501 16th Street, N.W.
Washington, D.C. 20011

Sixteenth Street Baptist Church, Inc.
5800 16th Street, N.W.
Washington, D.C. 20011

Soul Saving Center Church of God
1100 W Street, N.W.
Washington, D.C. 20009

Southern Baptist Church
134 L Street, N.W.
Washington, D.C. 20001

Southern Bethany Baptist Church
1001 Monroe Street, N.W.
Washington, D.C. 20010

Springfield Baptist Church
508 P Street, N.W.
Washington, D.C. 20001

St. Charles Baptist Church
4410 Georgia Avenue, N.W.
Washington, D.C. 20010

St. John United Baptist Church
6343 13th Street, N.W.
Washington, D.C. 20011

St. Joseph Baptist Church
1203 Emerson Street, N.W.
Washington, D.C. 20011

St. Luke Baptist Church
1415 Gallatian Street, N.W.
Washington, D.C. 20017

St. Mary's Baptist Church
8008 Eastern Avenue, N.W.
Washington, D.C. 20012

St. Mathews Overcoming Church
 of God
2110 14th Street, N.W.
Washington, D.C. 20009

St. Paul AME Zion Church
4901 14th Street, N.W.
Washington, D.C. 20011

St. Stephen's Baptist Church
628 M Street, N.W.
Washington, D.C. 20001

Star of Bethlehem COGIC
1435 Colorado Avenue, N.W.
Washington, D.C. 20001

Star of Hope COGIC
4607 14th Street, N.W.
Washington, D.C. 20011

Temple Baptist Church
3850 Nebraska Avenue, N.W.
Washington, D.C. 20016

Temple Church of God In Christ
1435 Park Road, N.W.
Washington, D.C. 20010

Tenth Street Baptist Church
1000 R Street, N.W.
Washington, D.C. 20001

The Church of God
1530 New Jersey Avenue, N.W.
Washington, D.C. 20001

The New Testament Church in Jesus Christ
39 Florida Avenue, N.W.
Washington, D.C. 20001

Third Baptist Church
1546 Fifth Street, N.W.
Washington, D.C. 20001

Third Street Church of God
1204 Third Street, N.W.
Washington, D.C. 20001

Third World and Peace Black Church
245 Peabody Street, N.W.
Washington, D.C. 20016

Trinity AME Zion Church
3505 16th Street, N.W.
Washington, D.C. 20010

True Gospel Baptist Church
1106 W Street, N.W.
Washington, D.C. 20009

True Grace Holy Temple Church
of Christ
205 V Street, N.W.
Washington, D.C. 20001

Turner Memorial AME Church
600 I Street, N.W.
Washington, D.C. 20001

United Holiness Church of Deliverance
825 Kennedy Street, N.W.
Washington, D.C. 20011

United House of Prayer for All People
601 M Street, N.W.
Washington, D.C. 20001

United True Love Gospel Mission
24 N Street, N.W.
Washington, D.C. 20001

Upperway Church
1600 llth Street, N.W.
Washington, D.C. 20001

Van Buren UM Church
35 Van Buren Street, N.W.
Washington, D.C. 20012

Verdadera Fe Baptist Church
1616 New Jersey Avenue, N.W.
Washington, D.C. 20001

Vermont Avenue Baptist Church
1630 Vermont Avenue Street, N.W.
Washington, D.C. 20009

Victory Memorial Baptist Church
316 Kennedy Street, N.W.
Washington, D.C. 20011

Walker Memorial Baptist Church
2020 13th Street, N.W.
Washington, D.C. 20009

Washington Apostolic Church
1436 Park Road, N.W.
Washington, D.C. 20010

Zion Baptist Church
4850 Blagden Avenue, N.W.
Washington, D.C. 20011

Zion Hill Baptist Church
841 Shepherd Street, N.W.
Washington, D.C. 20011

## CHURCHES - SOUTHEAST

A.P. Shaw United Methodist
2525 12th Street, S.E.
Washington, D.C. 20003

Ambassador Baptist Church
1412 Minnesota Avenue, S.E.
Washington, D.C. 20020

Anacostia Bible Church
16th Street & Minnesota Ave., S.E.
Washington, D.C. 20020

Apostolic Faith
5211 A Street, S.E.
Washington, D.C. 20019

Bethuel Temple Church of Christ
2406 Martin Luther King Ave., S.E.
Washington, D.C. 20020

Calvary Christian Church
909 11th Street, S.E.
Washington, D.C.

Campbell AME Church
2562 Martin Luther King Ave., S.E.
Washington, D.C. 20020

Capitol Hill UM Church
5th & Seward Square, S.E.
Washington, D.C. 20003

Central Baptist Church
3160 Pennsylvania Avenue, S.E.
Washington, D.C. 20020

Church of Jesus Christ
3458 Pennsylvania Avenue, S.E.
Washington, D.C. 20020

Church of the Holy Trinity
4628 Minnesota Avenue, S.E.
Washington, D.C. 20019

Covenant Baptist Church
3845 South Capitol Street, S.E.
Washington, D.C. 20032

Delaware Avenue Baptist Church
1301 V Street, S.E.
Washington, D.C. 20020

East Capitol Street Church of
 God In Christ
5026 East Capitol Street
Washington, D.C.

East Washington Heights Baptist Church
2220 Branch Avenue, S.E.
Washington, D.C. 20020

Ebenezer UM Church
4th & D Street, S.E.
Washington, D.C. 20013

Edgewood Baptist Church
3408 C Street, S.E.
Washington, D.C. 20019

Emanuel Baptist Church
2409 Ainger Place, S.E.
Washington, D.C. 20020

Evening Light Church of Christ
2812 Bruce Place, S.E.
Washington, D.C. 20020

Faith Baptist Church
9th and South Carolina Avenue, S.E.
Washington, D.C. 20003

Faith Tabernacle of Prayer
1601 23rd Street, S.E.
Washington, D.C. 20008

First Baptist Church
3440 Minnesota Avenue, S.E.
Washington, D.C. 20019

First Baptist Church of Marshall
 Heights
4934 B Street, S.E.
Washington, D.C. 20019

First National Baptist Church
5400 D Street, S.E.
Washington, D.C. 20019

First Rock Baptist Church
4630 Alabama Avenue, S.E.
Washington, D.C. 20019

First Rock Baptist Church
4373 G Street, S.E.
Washington, D.C. 20019

Four Gospel Baptist Church
1608 Massachusetts Avenue, S.E.
Washington, D.C. 20003

Galilee Baptist Church
2252 Minnesota Avenue, S.E.
Washington, D.C. 20020

Good Samaritan Baptist Church
5100 E Street, S.E.
Washington, D.C. 20019

Grace Apostolic Church
905 Alabama Avenue, S.E.
Washington, D.C. 20032

Grace Memorial Baptist Church
2407 Minnesota Avenue, S.E.
Washington, D.C. 20020

Greater Deliverance COGIC
441 Chaplin Street, S.E.
Washington, D.C. 20019

Greater People Union Baptist Church
1111 South Carolina Avenue, S.E.
Washington, D.C. 20003

Guiding Light Full Gospel Church
2627 Martin Luther King Ave., S.E.
Washington, D.C. 20020

Guiding Light Refuge Baptist Church
1 51st Street, S.E.
Washington, D.C. 20019

Harvey Memorial Baptist Church
3204 Brothers Place, S.E.
Washington, D.C. 20032

Holy Temple Church of Christ
439 12th Street, S.E.
Washington, D.C. 20003

I Am Church of God, Inc.
465 Valley Avenue, S.E.
Washington, D.C. 20032

Independent Church of God
2302 Ainger Place, S.E.
Washington, D.C. 20020

Israel Memorial Baptist Church
1911 Martin Luther King Ave., S.E.
Washington, D.C. 20020

Jesus Apostolic COGIC
2204 Martin Luther King Ave., S.E.
Washington, D.C. 20020

Jesus Christ of Power Church
3855 Halley Terrace, S.E.
Washington, D.C. 20032

Johenning Baptist Church
4025 9th Street, S.E.
Washington, D.C. 20023

199

Johnson Memorial Baptist Church
800 Ridge Road, S.E.
Washington, D.C. 20019

Jones Memorial UM Church
4625 G Street, S.E.
Washington, D.C. 20019

Liberty Baptist Church
527 Kentucky Avenue, S.E.
Washington, D.C. 20003

Macedonia Baptist Church
2625 Stanton Road, S.E.
Washington, D.C. 20020

Matthews Memorial Baptist Church
2616 Martin Luther King Ave., S.E.
Washington, D.C. 20020

Mentrotone Baptist Church
5211 B Street, S.E.
Washington, D.C. 20019

Mount Enon Missionary Baptist Church
1325 Branch Avenue, S.E.
Washington, D.C. 20020

Mount Ephraim Baptist Church
5713 Dix Street, S.E.
Washington, D.C. 20019

Mount Joy Baptist Church
514 Fourth Street, S.E.
Washington, D.C. 20003

Mount Calvary Baptist Church
801 North Carolina Avenue, S.E.
Washington, D.C. 20003

Mount Carmel Freewill Baptist Church
3001 N Street, S.E.
Washington, D.C. 20019

Mt. Calvary Evangelistic Church
2504 Naylor Road, S.E.
Washington, D.C. 20020

Mt. Moriah Baptist Church
1636 East Capitol Street, S.E.
Washington, D.C. 20003

Mt. Paran Baptist Church
1341 K Street, S.E.
Washington, D.C. 20003

Nationwide Unity Holy Church of God
2021 Martin Luther King Ave., S.E.
Washington, D.C. 20020

New Hope Freewill Baptist Church
754 11th Street, S.E.
Washington, D.C. 20003

New Image Community Baptist Church
1839 Alabama Avenue, S.E.
Washington, D.C. 20020

New Jerusalem Missionary
  Baptist Church
1736 Good Hope Road, S.E.
Washington, D.C. 20020

200

New Macedonia Baptist Church
4200 Massachusetts Avenue, S.E.
Washington, D.C. 20019

New Morning Star Baptist Church
1400 E Street, S.E.
Washington, D.C. 20003

New United Baptist Church
1401 South Carolina Avenue, S.E.
Washington, D.C. 20003

Open Door Baptist Church
136 56th Street, S.E.
Washington, D.C. 20019

Open Door Ministry
732 6th Street, S.E.
Washington, D.C. 20003

Paramount Baptist Church
3924 Fourth Street, S.E.
Washington, D.C. 20032

Pennsylvania Avenue Baptist Church
6000 Pennsylvania Avenue, S.E.
Washington, D.C. 20019

People's Church
535 8th Street, S.E.
Washington, D.C. 20003

Potomac Baptist Church
3340 Minnesota Avenue, S.E.
Washington, D.C. 20020

Prayer Temple Church
1259 K Street, S.E.
Washington, D.C. 20003

Providence Baptist Church
526 15th Street, S.E.
Washington, D.C. 20003

Rehoboth Baptist Church
621 Alabama Avenue, S.E.
Washington, D.C. 20020

Resurrection Baptist Church
3501 Martin Luther King Ave., S.E.
Washington, D.C. 20020

Revelation Baptist Church
2233 Hunter Place, S.E.
Washington, D.C. 20020

Ryland Epworth UM Church
3200 S Street, S.E.
Washington, D.C. 20020

Second St. James Baptist Church
2301 Minnesota Avenue, S.E.
Washington, D.C. 20020

Shiloh Apostolic Faith
2220 Martin Luther King Ave., S.E.
Washington, D.C. 20020

Southern Friendship Baptist Church
2600 Minnesota Avenue, S.E.
Washington, D.C. 20020

St. John CME Church
2801 Stanton Road, S.E.
Washington, D.C. 20020

St. Lucille AME Zion Church
5100 Astor Place, S.E.
Washington, D.C. 20019

St. Matthew's Baptist Church
1105 New Jersey Avenue, S.E.
Washington, D.C. 20003

Temple Missionary Baptist Church
3105 Martin Luther King Ave., S.E.
Washington, D.C. 20020

Thankful Baptist Church
1401 Independence Avenue, S.E.
Washington, D.C. 20003

Thomas Johns Memorial Baptist
  Church
13th and W Street, S.E.
Washington, D.C. 20003

Tried Stone Church of Christ
417 9th Street, S.E.
Washington, D.C. 20003

True Gospel Tabernacle Baptist Church
4201 Wheeler Road, S.E.
Washington, D.C. 20032

True Way Baptist Church
2417 Naylor Road, S.E.
Washington, D.C. 20020

Union Temple Baptist Church
2002 14th Street, S.E.
Washington, D.C. 20020

Unity of Love Praise Temple
3703 Martin Luther King Ave., S.E.
Washington, D.C. 20020

Universal Holiness Church
2426 Elvans Road, S.E.
Washington, D.C. 20020

Vineyard Baptist Church
401 16th Street, S.E.
Washington, D.C. 20003

Word of God Baptist Church
1512 K Street, S.E.
Washington, D.C. 20003

Young's Memorial Church of Christ
  Holiness
2490 Alabama Avenue, S.E.
Washington, D.C. 20020

### CHURCHES - SOUTHWEST

Bethel Pentecostal Tabernacle of
  the Assemblies of God
60 I Street, S.W.
Washington, D.C. 20024

Carron Baptist Church
1354 First Street, S.W.
Washington, D.C. 20024

Friendship Baptist Church
900 Delaware Avenue, S.W.
Washington, D.C. 20024

Redeemed Temple of Jesus Christ
734 1st Street, S.W.
Washington, D.C. 20024

Riverside Baptist Church
7th & Maine Avenue, S.W.
Washington, D.C. 20024

**MARYLAND CHURCHES**

Abyssinia Baptist Church
4705 Addison Road
Beaver Heights, Maryland 20743

Apostolic United Pentecostal Church
29 4th Street
Laurel, Maryland 20707

Ascension Baptist Church
4705 Deanwood Drive
Fairmont Heights, Maryland 20743

Assembly Church of our Lord Jesus
6020 Addison Road
Seat Pleasant, Maryland 20743

Bible Baptist Church of D.C.
6612 Gateway Boulevard
District Heights, Maryland 20747

Calvary Apostolic Church
222 Cedar Avenue
Gaithersburg, Maryland 20877

Capitol Heights CME Church
1112 Kayak Avenue
Capitol Heights, Maryland 20743

Carmody Hills Baptist Church
6501 Seat Pleasant Drive
Seat Pleasant, Maryland 20743

Christ Mission Church
5103 Nash Street
Chapel Oaks, Maryland 20743

Christ Temple Church of the Apostolic Faith, Inc.
2508 Kirtland Avenue
Forestville, Maryland 20747

Christ Outreach Temple
717 61st Avenue
Fairmont Heights, Maryland 20743

Christian Deliverance Fellowship
7612 Swan Terrace
Landover, Maryland 20785

Hope Christian Center
5301 Edgewood Road
College Park, Maryland 20748

Christian Tabernacle Holy Church
1201 Elsa Avenue
Landover, Maryland 20786

Church of Deliverance
1208 Clovis Avenue
Capitol Heights, Maryland 20743

Church of God of Prophecy
1709 Kenilworth Avenue
Capitol Heights, Maryland 20743

Church of God of Silver Spring
2108 Linden Lane
Silver Spring, Maryland 20906

Clinton AME Zion Church
1814 Westmore Avenue
Rockville, Maryland 20850

College Park Pentecostal Holiness Church
3828 University Boulevard East
College Park, Maryland 20742

Community Temple Church
6207 State Street
Cheverly, Maryland 20743

Craig Memorial Community Church
5305 Farmingdale Place
Capitol Heights, Maryland 20743

Crusader's Youth Revival Church
5722 George Palmer Highway
Seat Pleasant, Maryland 20743

Decatur Heights Baptist Church
4300 Edmonston Road
Bladensburg, Maryland 20710

Deliverance Church of Christ
500 Jadeleaf Avenue
Capitol Heights, Maryland 20743

Deliverance Temple Christian Church
354 Eastern Avenue
Mt. Rainier, Maryland 20743

Divine Mission Faith Bible Church
7111 Temple Hills Road
Camp Springs, Maryland 20748

East Side Holy Trinity Church, Inc.
717 58th Avenue
Fairmont Heights, Maryland 20743

Ebenezer AME Church
7806 Allentown Road
Fort Washington, Maryland 20744

Emmanuel Assembly
3506 Hubbard Avenue
Landover, Maryland 20785

Emmanuel Grace Tabernacle, Inc.
7300 Kent Town Drive
Landover, Maryland 20785

Faithful Holiness Church
4819 Marlboro Pike
Coral Hills, Maryland 20743

Faith Pentecostal Holiness Church
12619 Holdridge Road
Silver Spring, Maryland 20906

Faith Temple Number Two
5900 Addison Road
Seat Pleasant, Maryland 20743

Fellowship Baptist Church of Boulevard Heights
1608 Arcadia Avenue
Capitol Heights, Maryland 20743

Fidelity Christian Center
6811 F Street
Seat Pleasant, Maryland 20743

First Baptist Church of District Heights
7234 Lansdale Street
District Heights, Maryland 20747

First Baptist Church-Fairmont Heights
810 58th Avenue
Fairmont Heights, Maryland 20743

First Baptist Church of Glenarden
Glen Arden Pkwy & Brightseat Road
Glenarden, Maryland 20706

First Baptist Church of Guilford
7504 Oakland Mills Road
Columbia, Maryland 21046

First Baptist Church of Highland Park
6801 Sheriff Road
Landover, Maryland 20743

First Baptist Church of Hyattsville
5701 42nd Avenue
Hyattsville, Maryland 20781

First New Horizon Baptist Church
P.O. Box 176
Clinton, Maryland 20735

First Church of God of Fairmont Height
708 60th Avenue
Fairmont Heights, Maryland 20743

First United Pentecostal Church
5819 Kirby Road
Clinton, Maryland 20735

Free Gospel Church of Christ, Inc.
4703 Marlboro Pike
Coral Hills, Maryland 20743

Freedom Church
2916 East Avenue
Forestville, Maryland  20747

Freedom Way Baptist Church
1266 Benning Road
Capitol Heights, Maryland  20743

Friendship AOH Church of God
4814 Deanwood Drive
Deanwood Park, Maryland  20743

Full Gospel AME Zion Church
4207 Norcross Street
Temple Hills, Maryland  20748

Garden of Gethsemane Church Of God In Christ
4000 34th Street
Mt. Rainier, Maryland  20008

Gethsemane United Methodist Church
910 Addison Road South
Seat Pleasant, Maryland  20743

Glenarden Church of God In Christ
7939 Piedmont Avenue
Glenarden, Maryland  20743

Grace Temple COGIC
19 Lee Avenue
Takoma Park, Maryland  20906

Grace United Methodist Church
716 59th Avenue
Fairmont Heights, Maryland  20743

Greater Church of Deliverance
5927 Central Avenue
Capitol Heights, Maryland  20743

Greater Mt. Nebo AME Zion Church
17214 Queen Anne Road
Upper Marlboro, Maryland  20772

Haitian Baptist Mission
832 Wayne Avenue
Silver Spring, Maryland  20910

Harvest Church International, Inc.
2211 Varnum Street
Mt. Rainier, Maryland  20712

Hemingway Memorial AME Church
5252 Addison Road
Chapel Oaks, Maryland  20703

Holy Trinity All Denom. House of Prayer
901 Cedar Heights Drive
Capitol Heights, Maryland  20743

Hunter Memorial AME Church
5OOl Holly Spring Street, S.E.
Dupont Heights, Maryland  20006

Independent Church of Christ
5500 Jefferson Drive
Fairmont Heights, Maryland  20743

Interdenominational Church of Christ
P.O. Box 1206
Landover, Maryland  20706

Interdenominational Church of God
14 Brooks Avenue
Gaithersburg, Maryland 20877

International Church of Christ Ministry
P.O. Box 1206
Landover, Maryland 20785

Jordan Baptist Church
5034 Emo Street
Capitol Heights, Maryland 20743

Lighthouse Church
5201 Baltimore Lane
Lanham-Seabrook, Maryland 20706

Lighthouse Church
6811 F Street
Seat Pleasant, Maryland 20003

Lighthouse Full Gospel Mission Church
5927 Central Avenue
Seat Pleasant, Maryland 20743

Little Child Holy Church On The Rock
6044 Central Avenue
Capitol Heights, Maryland 20743

Living Word Church of God In Christ
7300 Kent Town Drive
Landover, Maryland 20785

Love Temple Church of Deliverance
3510 Rhode Island Avenue
Mt. Rainier, Maryland 20781

Macedonia Baptist Church
5119 River Road
Bethesda, Maryland 20816

Maple Springs Baptist Church
4131 Belt Road
Boulevard Heights, Maryland 20743

Metro World Outreach Center
1312 Larchmont Avenue
Capitol Heights, Maryland 20743

Mt. Airy Full Gospel Church
13949 Penn Shop Road
Mt. Airy, Maryland 21771

Mt. Ararat Baptist Church
2005 Dupont Avenue
Suitland, Maryland 20746

Mt. Ennon Baptist Church
9832 Piscataway Road
Clinton, Maryland 20735

Mt. Pisgah AME Church
8651 Old Annapolis Road
Columbia, Maryland 21045

National Apostolic Church
10002 Sutherland Road
Silver Spring, Maryland 20910

New Covenant Church
5405 36th Avenue
Hyattsville, Maryland 20782

New Haven Baptist Church
7611 Piney Branch Road
Silver Spring, Maryland 20910

New Hope Baptist Church
3400 Pinevale Avenue
Forestville, Maryland 20747

New Life Full Gospel Baptist Church
3814 Old Silver Hill Road
Suitland, Maryland 20746

New St. James United Holy Church
3929 Allison Street
Brentwood, Maryland 20722

New Testament Church
6737 Annapolis Road
Landover, Maryland 20784

Newborn Church of God In Christ
726 60th Place
Fairmont Heights, Maryland 20743

One Way United Holiness Church
5348 Sheriff Road
Chapel Oaks, Maryland 20743

Outreach Christian Center
4927 Suitland Road
Suitland, Maryland 20743

Overcomers Gospel Church
3623 Eastern Avenue
Mt. Rainier, Maryland 20743

Parker Memorial Baptist Church
111 Geneva Avenue
Silver Spring, Maryland 20910

Parkview Baptist Church
7900 Oxman Road
Landover, Maryland 20706

Parkway Baptist Church
6809 District Heights Parkway
District Heights, Maryland 20747

Peaceful Bible Baptist Church
6076 Central Avenue
Capitol Heights, Maryland 20743

Pentecostal Evangelical Church
7711 Allendale Drive
Palmer Park, Maryland 20743

Pentecostal Holiness Church
4915 Wheeler Road
Oxon Hill, Maryland 20743

Redeeming Love Christian Center
8741 Fairhaven Place
Laurel, Maryland 20707

Refreshing Springs COGIC
6200 Riverdale Road
Riverdale, Maryland 20737

Refuge Church of Christ
Laytonsville Road
Olney, Maryland 20832

Refuge Baptist Church
4104 23rd Place
Temple Hills, Maryland 20748

Revelation Baptist Church
6195 Central Avenue
Capitol Heights, Maryland 20743

Ridgely Church of God In Christ
9235 D-Arcy Road
Forestville, Maryland 20747

Righteous Church of Holiness Inc.
5500 Jefferson Heights Drive
Fairmont Heights, Maryland 20743

Round Oak Baptist Church
15812 Good Hope Road
Silver Spring, Maryland 20904

Sacred Hour Full Gospel
1022 58th Avenue
Fairmont Heights, Maryland 20743

Scotland AME Zion Church
10902 Seven Locks Road
Rockville, Maryland 20854

Seat Pleasant Baptist Church
5948 Addison Road
Seat Pleasant, Maryland 20743

Seaton Memorial AME Church
5507 Lincoln Avenue
Lanham-Seabrook, Maryland 20706

Sermon on the Mount
5606 Marlboro Pike
District Heights, Maryland 20747

Shekinah Worship Center
5125 Norbeck Road
Rockville, Maryland 20853

Shiloh Baptist Church
8801 Ardwick-Ardmore Road
Landover, Maryland 20706

Shining Star Baptist Church
5737 George Palmer Highway
Capitol Heights, Maryland 20743

Solid Rock Church
5401 Good Luck Road
Riverdale, Maryland 20737

Spirit of Peace Baptist Church
4105 Alton Street
Capitol Heights, Maryland 20743

Spirit of Peace Baptist Church
4106 Byers Street
Capitol Heights, Maryland 20743

Spirit of Peace Baptist Church
7600 Willow Hill Drive
Landover, Maryland 20706

Spirit of Peace Baptist Church
4311 R Street
Capitol Heights, Maryland 20743

St. Paul Baptist Church
1608 Arcadia Avenue
Boulevard Heights, Maryland 20743

St. John Baptist De LaSalle
5706 Sargeant Road
Chillum, Maryland 20782

Straight Way Church of Christ
1723 Kenilworth Avenue
Beaver Heights, Maryland 20743

Sylvan Vista Baptist Church
1103 60th Avenue
Fairmont Heights, Maryland 20743

Temple Church of God In Christ
65 Spa Road
Annapolis, Maryland 21401

Tree of Life Fellowship
1400 Doewood Lane
Capitol Heights, Maryland 20743

True Deliverance Church of God
1804 Quarter Avenue
Capitol Heights, Maryland 20743

United Fellowship Church
8501 Houston Street
Silver Spring, Maryland 20910

United Holiness Deliverance Church
6209 Eastern Avenue
Hyattsville, Maryland 20743

Victory Temple
6608 Seat Pleasant Drive
Seat Pleasant, Maryland 20743

Wayside Holiness Church Assembly of God
1907 Columbia Avenue
Landover, Maryland 20785

Way of Life Church of Christ
3014 St. Clair Drive
Temple Hills, Maryland

Word Christian Center
3401 Rhode Island
Mt. Rainier, Maryland 20712

Youth for Christ Mission
1218 Hill Road
Highland Park, Maryland 20777

Zion Church of Jesus Christ Apostolic
Mt. Harmony Run
Owings, Maryland 20736

Zion Baptist Church
2626 Kent Village Drive
Landover, Maryland 20785

**VIRGINIA CHURCHES**

Abundant Life United Holy Church
204 E. Del Ray Avenue
Alexandria, Virginia 22301

Aldersgate United Methodist Church
Fort Hunt Road & Collingwood Road
Alexandria, Virginia 22308

Alfred Street Baptist Church
301 South Alfred Street
Alexandria, Virginia 22314

Antioch Church of Christ
1120 Queen Street
Alexandria, Virginia 22314

Asbury United Methodist Church
P.O. Box 1122
Middleburg, Virginia

Baptist Temple Baptist
700 Commonwealth Avenue
Alexandria, Virginia 22301

Bethlehem Baptist Church
7836 Fordson Road
Alexandria, Virginia 22306

Beulah Baptist Church
320 South Washington Street
Alexandria, Virginia 22314

Bibleway Church of our Lord Jesus
4340 Ox Road
Fairfax, Virginia 22030

Bridal Call of Christ Church
5011 South Eighth Road
Arlington, Virginia 22204

Church of God of Prophecy
6409 Telegraph Road
Alexandria, Virginia

Crossroads Baptist Church
3530 Moncure Avenue
Baileys Crossroads, Virginia

Ebenezer Baptist Church
301 North Patrick Street
Alexandria, Virginia 22314

Ebenezer Baptist Church
909 Queen Street
Alexandria, Virginia 22314

Galloway United Methodist Church
304 Annandale Road
Falls Church, Virginia 22042

Gethsemane Church of God In Christ
130 North Fayette
Alexandria, Virginia 22314

Golden Church of God of Prophecy
3511 South Kemper Road
Arlington, Virginia

Lomax AME Zion Church
2706 24th Road South
Arlington, Virginia 22206

Love of Christ Church
1505 Mount Vernon Avenue
Alexandria, Virginia 22301

Macedonia Baptist Church
3412 22nd South
Arlington, Virginia 22204

Mead Memorial Episcopal Church
322 North Alfred Street
Alexandria, Virginia 22314

Mount Calvary Holy Church of America
600 North Columbus Street
Alexandria, Virginia 22314

Mount Ne-Bo Pentecostal Church
2300 Burke Avenue
Alexandria, Virginia 22301

Mount Olive Baptist Church
1601 South 13th Road
Arlington, Virginia 22204

Mount Olivet United Methodist Church
1500 North Glebe Road
Arlington, Virginia 22207

Mount Pleasant Baptist Church
6477 Lincolnia Road
Alexandria, Virginia 22312

Mount Salvation Baptist Church
1961 North Culpeper Street
Arlington, Virginia 22207

New Apostolic Church
21 North Quacker Lane
Alexandria, Virginia 22304

New Life Open Bible Church
6434 Franconia Road
Springfield, Virginia 22150

Roberts Memorial UM Church
604 South Washington Street
Alexandria, Virginia 22314

Russell Temple CME Church
507 North Alfred
Alexandria, Virginia 22314

Shiloh Baptist Church
1404 Duke Street
Alexandria, Virginia 22314

Ship of Zion Church
P.O. Box 1952
Alexandria, Virginia 22313

St. Paul Pentecostal Church
3305 Mount Vernon Avenue
Alexandria, Virginia 22305

St. Paul Pentecostal United Holy
Church of America, Inc.
3305 East Clifford Avenue
Alexandria, Virginia 22305

Third Baptist Church
917 Princess Street
Alexandria, Virginia  22314

United Faith Pentecostal Church
205 East Mount Ida Avenue
Alexandria, Virginia  22301

United Pentecostal Church
2100 North Quebec
Arlington, Virginia  22207

United Pentecostal Church of Herndon
720 Grant Street
Herndon, Virginia  22070

Warner Baptist
3613 Lacy Boulevard
Falls Church, Virginia   22041

Woodlawn United Methodist Church
7730 Fordson Road
Alexandria, Virginia  22306

# *PART III*
# *ECUMENICAL ORGANIZATIONS AND SERVICE AGENCIES*

## ARTS ORGANIZATIONS

Alexandria Society for the Pre-
servation of Black Heritage
638 North Alfred Street
Alexandria, Virginia 22314

African American Museums Association
420 Seventh Street, N.W.
Washington, D.C. 20004

Association for the Study of Afro-
American Life and History, Inc.
1401 Fourteenth Street, N.W.
Washington, D.C. 20005

S.E. Cultural Institute for the Arts
1501 T Street, S.E.
Washington, D.C. 20020

## BOOKSTORES

Alpha & Omega Christian Bookstore
3466 14th Street, N.W.
Washington, D.C. 20010

Battle's Religious Bookstore
4311 Sheriff Road, N.E.
Washington, D.C. 20019

Free Gospel Bible Bookstore
4711 Marlboro Pike
Coral Hills, Maryland 20743

Gospel Notes
6147 Oxon Hill Road
Oxon Hill, MD  20745

Harvest Church International
2211 Varnum Street
Mt. Rainier, MD  20712

New Bethel COGIC Bookstore
6440 Piney Branch Road
Washington, D.C. 20012

Rejoice Christian Store
5682 Silver Hill Road
District Heights, MD  20747

Rock's Uniform & Christian Bookstore
1104 H Street, N.E.
Washington, D.C. 20002

Time Tunnel Bookstore
1116 H Street, N.E.
Washington, D.C.  20002

Unlimited Faith Christian Bookstore
441 Kennedy Street, N.W.
Washington, D.C. 20011

## COLLEGES AND SEMINARIES

Bowie State College
Bowie, Maryland 20715

Choppin State College
Baltimore, Maryland 21216

District of Columbia Teachers College
Washington, D.C. 20009

Federal City College
Washington, D.C. 20005

Hampton Institute
Hampton, Virginia 23368

Howard University
2400 Sixth Street, N.W.
Washington, D.C. 20001

University of District of Columbia
4200 Connecticut Avenue, N.W.
Washington, D.C. 20008

Washington Baptist Seminary
1600 13th Street, N.W.
Washington, D.C.  20009

## COUNSELLING SERVICES

Hopkins House Association, Inc.
1224 Princess Street
Alexandria, Virginia 22314

National Black Child Development Institute
1463 Rhode Island Avenue, N.W.
Washington, D.C. 20005

## ECUMENICAL AGENCIES

Africun-American Women's Clergy Association
P.O. Box 1493
Washington, D.C. 20013

Baptist Convention for Wash., D.C.
1628 16th Street, N.W.
Washington, D.C. 20009

Baptist Joint Committee on Public Affairs
200 Maryland Avenue, N.E.
Washington, D.C. 20002

Christian Star Enterprises, Inc.
P.O. Box 531403
Forestville, Maryland 20753

Congress of National Black Churches
1225 I Street, N.W., Suite 750
Washington, D.C. 20005

DC Baptist Convention Headquarters
1628 16th Street, N.W.
Washington, D.C. 20009

District of Columbia Bible Institute
501 V Street, S.E.
Washington, D.C. 20019

Ecumenical Campus Ministry of UDC
900 Massachusetts Avenue, N.W.
Washington, D.C. 20001

Fellowship of Christian Athletes
134 Michigan Avenue, N.E.
Washington, D.C. 20017

Interdenominational Church Ushers
1923 16th Street, N.W.
Washington, D.C. 20009

National Association of Pastoral Musicians
1029 Vermont Avenue, N.W.
Washington, D.C. 20005

National Treasurers of Religious Institutes
8824 Cameron Street
Silver Spring, Maryland 20910

National Fellowship Program for
  Black Pastors
1225 I Street, N.W., Suite 750
Washington, D.C. 20005

National United Church Ushers Association
1431 Shepherd Street, N.W.
Washington, D.C. 20011

Successful Stewardship for Life Ministries, Inc.
1526 East Capitol Street, N.E.
Washington, D.C. 20003

United Outreach for Christ Mission Team
P.O. Box 56035
Washington, D.C. 20011

Wednesday Clergy Fellowship
1325 Maryland Avenue, N.E.
Washington, D.C. 20002

## EDUCATIONAL ORGANIZATIONS

Black Church Project-AAAS
1333 H Street, N.W.
Washington, D.C. 20005

Black Scholars Education Projects
930 F Street, N.W.
Washington, D.C. 20004

## FUNDING ORGANIZATIONS

Black Student Fund
3636 16th Street, N.W.
Washington, D.C. 20010

Minority Broadcast Investment and Fund
1155 Connecticut Ave., N.W.
Washington, D.C. 20036

MBE Legal Defense and Education Fund
318 Massachusetts Ave., N.E.
Washington, D.C. 20002

Minority Legislative Education Program
2030 M Street, N.W.
Washington, D.C. 20036

Miss Black USA Scholarship Foundation
113 69th Street
Seat Pleasant, Maryland 20743

Philanthropy and the Black Church Project
Council on Foundations
1828 L Street, N.W.
Washington, D.C. 20036-5168\

## PROFESSIONAL BUSINESS ORGANIZATIONS

American Association of Black Women
  Entrepreneurs
1326 Missouri Avenue, N.W., #4
Washington, D.C. 20011

Anacostia Information Center
2605 Wade Road, S.E.
Washington, D.C. 20020

Black Entertainment Network
1232 31st Street, N.W.
Washington, D.C. 20007

Blacks In Government
1424 K Street, N.W., #604
Washington, D.C. 20005

Black Nurses Association
1205 Geranium Street, N.W.
Washington, D.C. 20012

Black Silent Majority Committee
325 Pennsylvania Avenue, S.E.
Washington, D.C. 20003

Black Women United for Action
P.O. Box 1138
Centreville, Virginia 22021

Consortium of Musicians of the
 Metropolitan Area, Inc.
P.O. Box 0469
Temple Hills, MD 20748

D.C. Federation of Musicians
Local 161-710
5020 Wisconsin Avenue, N.W.
Washington, D.C. 20016

Dept. of Minority and Special Services
National Association of Broadcasters
1771 N Street, N.W.
Washington, D.C. 20036

Gospelrama Gospel Expo
P.O. Box 1342
Washington, D.C. 20013

International Praise Gospel Music
 Workshop
1985 Glencrest Lane
Annapolis, MD 21401

Jade Production
P.O. Box 7772
Washington, D.C. 20044

Joan Hillsman Music Network
P.O. Box 10193
Washington, D.C. 20018

John Ray Associates
1425 K Street, N.W., #1007
Washington, D.C. 20005

Middle Atlantic Regional Press
100 Bryant Street, N.W.
Washington, D.C. 20001

Minority Business and Professional
 Directory
1110 4th Street, N.W.
Washington, D.C. 20001

Minority Business Resources
 Institute of Prince Georges County
9200 Basil Court, Suite 209
Landover, Maryland 20785

Minority Media Syndicate, Inc.
1025 Vermont Avenue, N.W.
Washington, D.C.  20005

Minority Services
1925 K Street, N.W.
Washington, D.C.  20006

Miss Caribbean Padgent
6616 Allegheny Avenue
Takoma Park, Maryland  20912

National Association of Black Entrepreneurs
1377 K Street, N.W., Suite 616
Washington, D.C. 20006

National Association for Equal
  Opportunity in Higher Education
2243 Wisconsin Avenue, N.W.
Washington, D.C. 20007

National Association of Neighborhoods
1651 Fuller Street, N.W.
Washington, D.C. 20009

National Black Caucus of State Legislators
444 North Capitol Street, N.W.
Washington, D.C.  20001

National Black Media Coalition
38 New York Avenue, N.W.
Washington, D.C.  20001

National Dental Association
5506 Connecticut Avenue, N.W., #24-25
Washington, D.C.  20015

National Urban Coalition
1120 G Street, N.W., 9th Floor
Washington, D.C. 20005

Black Attorney's Association of NVA
807-809 Franklin Street
Alexandria, Virginia 22314

Northern Virginia Branch of the
  Washington Urban League, Inc.
1321 Cameron Street
Alexandria, Virginia 22314

Saunders B. Moon Community Association
8100 Fordson Road, Box 6039
Alexandria, Virginia 22306

Sideburn Civic Association, Inc.
Eighth District Black Caucus
10133 Zion Drive
Fairfax, Virginia  22032

## RADIO STATIONS

WDCU (90.1 FM)
4200 Connecticut Avenue, N.W.
Washington, D.C. 20008

WHUR (93.3 FM)
529 Bryant Street, N.W.
Washington, D.C. 20059

WOL (1450 AM)
1680 Wisconsin Avenue, N.W.
Washington, D.C. 20002

WYCB (1340 AM)
529 14th Street, N.W., Suite 228
Washington, D.C. 20045

## RELIGIOUS GOODS

G&C Church Supplies
1910 4th Street, N.E.
Washington, D.C.  20002

Hoffman Brothers Robe Co., Inc.
c/o Johnell Powell
9015 Longbow Road
Fort Washington, MD  20744

Northeast Religious Supplies
711 H Street, N.E.
Washington, D.C.  20002

Pursell's Church Supplies, Inc.
401 M Street, S.W.
Washington, D.C.  20024

# SECTION IV

# APPENDIX

# BIBLIOGRAPHY

1986. A Rage for Order: Black/White Relations in the American South Since Emancipation. New York: Oxford Univ. Press.

1985. The Liturgical Ministry of Deacons. Collegeville, Minn.: Liturgical Press.

1984b. No Chariot Let Down: Charleston's Free People of Color on the Eve of the Civil War. Chapel Hill: Univ. of North Carolina Press.

1977. "Religious Affiliation and Militancy among Urban Blacks: Some Catholic/Protestant Comparisons." Social Science Quarterly 57 (Mar. 1977): 821-32.

Andrews, William. 1986a. To Tell a Free Story: The First Century of Afro-American Autobiography, 1760-1865. Urbana: Univ. of Illinois Press.

Arscott, Lindsay A. 1986. "Black Theology," Evangelical Review of Theology 10.

Baer, H.A., & M. Singer. 1992. African American Religion in the 20th Century -- Varieties of Protest and Accommodation. Knoxville: University of Tennessee Press.

Baer, Hans. 1984. The Black Spiritual Movement: A Religious Response to Racism. Knoxville: Univ. of Tennessee Press.

Bailey, Kenneth. 1964. Southern White Protestantism in the Twentieth Century. New York: Harper & Row.

Baldwin, James. 1953. Go Tell It on the Mountain. New York: Signet.

Baldwin, Lewis V. 1992. To Make the Wounded Whole: The Cultural Legacy of Martin Luther King, Jr.; Minneapolis, MN: Fortress Press.

Banks, William L. 1972. The Black Church in the U.S. Chicago: Moody Press.

Banner-Haley, Charles Pete T. 1994. The Fruits of Integration: Black Middle-Class Ideology and Culture, 1960-1990; University Press of Mississippi.

Billingsley, Andrew. 1968. Black Families in White America. Englewood Cliffs, N.J.: Prentice-Hall.

Blassingame, John W. 1972. The Slave Community. New York: Oxford Univ. Press.

Bossy, John. 1985. Christianity in the West, 1400-1700. New York: Oxford Univ. Press.

Bowman, Thea. 1987. "Let the Church Say 'Amen!'" Extension 81, no. 9 (Mar.-Apr.): 10-11.

Brantl, George, ed. 1962. Catholicism. New York: George Braziller.

Carroll, Charles. 1900. "The Negro a Beast" or "In the Image of God." St. Louis: American Book and Bible Society.

Cleage, Albert B. 1969. The Black Messiah. New York: Sheed and Ward.

Cone, James. 1993. Black Theology; A Documentary History. Maryknoll: Orbis.

Cone, James H. 1986. "Black Theology in American Religion," Theology Today 43.

Cone, James H. 1975. God of the Oppressed. New York: Seabury Press.

Cone, James H. 1973. "Black Theology and Black Liberation," in Black Theology: The South African Voice, ed. Basil Moore. London: C. Hurst & Co.

Cone, James H. 1970. A Black Theology of Liberation. Philadelphia: J. P. Lippencott.

Cone, James H. 1969. Black Theology and Black Power. New York: Seabury.

Cone, James H. 1966-1979. "The White Church and Black Power," in G. S. Wilmore and J. H. Cone, Black Theology: A Documentary History. Maryknoll, NY: Orbis.

Conzelmann, Hans. 1973. History of Primitive Christianity. Nashville, Tenn.: Abingdon.

Copeland, Shawn. 1989. "African American Catholics and Black Theology: An Interpretation." Wilmore, ed., African American Religious Studies. 228-49.

David, Jay. 1968. Growing Up Black. New York: William Morrow and Sons.

Davis, Gerald. 1985. I Got the Word in Me and I Can Sing It You Know: A Study of the Performed African-American Sermon. Philadelphia: Univ. of Pennsylvania Press.

Douglas, Kelly Brown. 1994. The Black Christ. Maryknoll, NY: Orbis.

Downing, Frederick. 1986. To See the Promised Land: The Faith Pilgrimmages of Martin Luther King, Jr. Macon: Mercer UP.

English, James W. 1970.  "Could Racism Be Hereditary?", Eternity, September.

Erickson, Millard J. 1983. Christian Theology. Grand Rapids: Baker Book House.

Evans, Anthony T. 1977. Biblical Theology and the Black Experience Dallas: Black Evangelistic Enterprise.

Evans, James H. 1992. We Have Been Believers: An African-American Systematic Theology. Minneapolis, MN: Fortress Press.

Farajaje-Jones, Elias. 1990. In Search of Zion: The Spiritual Significance of Africa in Black Religious Movements. New York: P. Lang.

Findlay, James F. 1993. Church People in the Struggle:The National Council of Churches and The Black Freedom Movement, 1950-1970. New York:  Oxford University Press.

First African Baptist Church. 1977. "One Hundred Eighty-Ninth Birthday." Pamphlet. Georgia Historical Society, Savannah.

Fitts, Leroy. 1985. A History of Black Baptists. Nashville, Tenn.: Broadman Press.

Frazier, E. Franklin. 1963. The Negro Church in America. New York: Schocken Books.

Freedman, Samuel G. 1993. Upon This Rock: The Miracles of a Black Church. New York: Harper Collins.

Friedman, Lawrence J. 1970. The White Savage: Racial Fantasies in the Postbellum South. Englewood Cliffs, N.J.: Prentice-Hall.

Gadsden, R. W. 1969. "A Brief History of the First Congregational Church, United Church of Christ, Savannah GA, April 1869-April 1969." Mimeo.

225

Gates, Jr., Henry Louis, and Cornel West. 1996. The Future of the Trace. New York: Knopf.

Gilpin, Clark, W., 1990. ed. Public Faith: Reflections on the Political Role of American Churches. St. Louis, MO: CBP Press.

Gutman, Herbert. 1976. The Black Family in Slavery and Freedom, 1750-1925. New York: Random House.

Hamilton, Charles V. 1972. The Black Preacher in America. New York: William Morrow.

Harris, Forrest E. 1993. Ministry for Social Crisis: Theology and Praxis in the Black Church Tradition. Macon, GA: Mercer University Press.

Harris, Forrest E. and Donna E. Allen. 1993. A Call to a National Dialogue and Reflection on What Does It Mean to be Black and Christian. Vanderbilt Univ. Divinity School, Nashville, TN.

Harris, James H. 1991. Pastoral Theology: A Black-Church Perspective. Minneapolis, MN: Fortress Press.

Harris, J.H. 1987. Black Ministers and Laity in the Urban Church: An Analysis of Political and Social Expectations. Lanham, MD: University Press of America.

Henri, Florette. 1975. Black Migration: Movement North 1900-1920. Garden City, N.Y.: Doubleday.

Herskovits, Melville. 1958. The Myth of the Negro Past. Boston: Beacon.

Hood, Robert E. 1990. Must God Remain Greek: Afro Cultures and God-Talk. Minneapolis, MN : Fortress Press.

Hooks, Bell. 1990. Yearning: Race, Gender and Cultural Politics. Boston: South End Press.

Hopkins, Dwight N. 1993. Shoes That Fit Our Feet: Sources for a Constructive Black Theology. Maryknoll, NY: Orbis Books.

Hopkins, Dwight N. and George C. L. Cummings, eds. 1991. Cut Loose Your Stammering Tongue: Black Theology in the Slave Narratives. Maryknoll, NY: Orbis Books.

Hopkins, Dwight N. et al. 1990. Black Theology in the Slave Narratives. (Sound recording proceedings of the Black Theology Consultation of the Hopkins, America Academy of Religion).

House, H. Wayne. 1982. "An Investigation of Black Liberation Theology," Bibliotheca Sacra.

James, Stanlie M. and Abena P.A., Busia, eds. 1993. Theorizing Black Feminisms: The Visionary Pragmatism of Black Women. New York: Routledge, London.

Johnson, Daniel M., and Rex R. Campbell. 1981. Black Migration in America. Durham: Duke Univ. Press.

Johnson, James W. [1927] 1965. Autobiography of an Ex-Colored Man. New York: Hearst Corp.

Johnson, James W., and J. Rosamund Johnson. [1923-24] 1953-54. The Book of American Negro Spirituals. New York: Da Capo.

Johnson, Michael P., and James L. Roark. 1984a. Black Masters: A Free Family of Color in the Old South. New York: W. W. Norton.

Jones, D.J., and W.H. Matthews. 1977. The Black Church: A Community Resource -- a selection of papers from a conference titled "The Religious Experiences of Afro-Americans" held at Howard University, Washington, D.C., June 3-5, 1976. Washington, D.C.: Institute for Urban Affairs and Research, Howard University.

Jones, Major. 1987. The Color of God: The Concept of God in Afro-American Thought. Macon: Mercer UP.

Joyner, Charles. 1984. Down by the Riverside: A South Carolina Slave Community. Urbana: Univ. of Illinois Press.

Kebede, Asherafi. 1982. Roots of Black Music. Englewood Cliffs, N.J.: Prentice-Hall.

Keener, Craig S. and Glenn Usry. 1996. Black Man's Religion: Can Christianity Be Afrocentric?. New York: InterVarsity Press.

Kunnie, Julian. 1994. Models of Black Theology: Issues in Class, Culture, and Gender. Valley Forge, PA: Trinity Press International.

Kwatera, Michael. 1982. The Ministry of Servers. Collegeville, Minn.: Liturgical Press.

Lawrence, Beverly Hall. 1996. Reviving the Spirit. New York: Grove Press.

Lebsock, Suzanne. 1993. Righteous Discontent: The Women's Movement in the Black Baptist Church, 1880-1920. The New York Times Books Review.

Lester, James A. 1972. A History of the Georgia Baptist Convention, 1822-1972. Nashville, Tenn.: Curley.

Levine, Lawrence. 1977. Black Culture and Black Consciousness: Afro-American Folk Thought from Slavery to Freedom. New York: Oxford Univ. Press.

Lincoln, C. Eric and Lawrence H. Mamiya. 1990. The Black Church in the African-American Experience. Durham: Duke University Press.

Lincoln, C. Eric. 1973. "The Development of Black Religion in America."

Love, E. K. 1888. History of the First African Baptist Church from Its Organization January 20 1788 to July 1 1888 Including the Centennial Celebration, Addresses, Sermons, etc. Savannah: Morning Newsprint.

Lovell, John. 1972. Black Song: The Forge and the Flame. New York: Paragon House.

Marks, Carole. 1989. Farewell--We're Good and Gone: The Great Black Migration. Bloomington: Indiana University Press.

Martey, Emmanuel. 1993. African Theology: Inculturation and Liberation. Maryknoll, NY: Orbis.

Marx, Gary. 1967. "Religion: Opiate or Inspiration of Civil Rights Militancy among Negroes?" American Sociological Review 32 (Feb.): 64-72.

Mathews, Donald G. 1977. Religion in the Old South. Chicago: University of Chicago Press.

McCall, Emmanuel. 1976. "Black Liberation Theology: A Politics of Freedom," Review and Expositor 73.

McClain, William B. 1990. Come Sunday: The Liturgy of Zion. Nashville: Abingdon Press.

McKenna, Edward. 1983. The Ministry of Musicians. Collegeville, Minn.: Liturgical Press.

Means, Howard. 1986. "God Is Back." The Washingtonian. Dec.: 150-69.

Meeks, Wayne. 1983. The First Urban Christians: The Social World of the Apostle Paul. New Haven: Yale Univ. Press.

Meier, August, and Elliott Rudwick. 1986. Black History and the Historical Profession, 1915-1980. Urbana: Univ. of Illinois Press.

Meshack, B.A. 1976. Is the Baptist Church relevant to the Black Community? San Francisco: R and E Research Associates.

Mitchell, Henry H. 1979. Black Preaching. San Francisco: Harper & Row.

Moloney, Francis J. 1990. A Body Broken for a Broken People. Melbourne, Australia: Collins Dove.

Morris, Calvin 1990. Reverdy Ransom: Black Advocate of the Social Gospel. Lanham, MD: Univ. Press of America.

Moses, Wilson J. 1978. The Golden Age of Black Nationalism, 1850-1925. Hamden, Conn.: Shoe String Press. Rpt. New York: Oxford Univ. Press, 1988.

Mukenge, I.R. 1983. The Black Church in Urban America: A Case Study in Political Economy. Lanham, MD: University Press of America.

Murphy, Larry G. 1993. Encyclopedia of African American Religions. New York: Garland.

Myers, Lewis. 1833. "Origins and Progress of Methodism in Savannah." Methodist Magazine and Quarterly Review 15: 246-56.

Myers, William H. 1994. God's Yes Was Louder than My No: Rethinking the African-American Call to Ministry. Grand Rapids, MI: W B Eerdmans.

Myrdal, Gunnar. 1944. An American Dilemma: The Negro Problem and Modern Democracy. New York: Harper & Row.

Newman, Susan. 1996. With Heart and Hand: The Black Church Working to Save Black Children. Nashville, Tennessee: Judson Press.

Nicolson, Ronald. 1990. A Black Future?: Jesus and Salvation in South Africa. Valley Forge, PA: Trinity International Press.

Ochs, Stephen. 1990. Desegregating the Altar. Baton Rouge: Louisiana State Univ. Press.

Paris, P.J. 1985. The Social Teaching of the Black Churches. Philadelphia: Fortress Press.

Paris, Arthur. 1982. Black Pentecostalism; Southern Religion in an Urban World. Amherst: U of Massachusetts P.

Paris, Peter. 1991. Black Religious Leaders; Conflict in Unity. Louisville: Westminster.

Payne, W.J. 1995. Directory of African-American Religious Bodies: A Compendium by the Howard University School of Divinity. Washington, D.C.: Howard University Press.

Perdue, Robert. 1973. The Negro in Savannah, 1865-1900. New York: Exposition Press.

Pityana, Nyameko. 1973. "What Is Black Consciousness?" Black Theology: The South African Voice, ed. Basil Moore. London: C. Hurst & Co.

Pozzetta, George, and Randall Miller, eds. 1988. Shades of the Sunbelt: Essays on Ethnicity, Race, and the Urban South. New York: Greenwood Press.

Price, Richard. 1984. First-Time: The Historical Vision of an Afro-American People. Baltimore: Johns Hopkins Univ. Press.

Raboteau, Albert. 1978. Slave Religion: The Invisible Institution in the Antebellum South. London: Oxford Univ. Press.

Raines, Howell. 1977. My Soul Is Rested: Movement Days in the Deep South Remembered. New York: Putnam Books.

Roberts, DeOtis. 1971. Liberation and Reconciliation: A Black Theology (Philadelphia: Westminster Press.

Roll, Jordan. 1974. The World the Slaves Made. New York: Random House.

Russell, H. 1981. Africa's Twelve Apostles. Boston: Daughters of St. Paul.

Salley, Columbus, and Ronal Behm. 1988. What Color Is Your God? Black Consciousness and Christian Faith. Secaucus, N.J.: Citadel Press.

Simms, James M. 1888. The First Baptist Church in North America. Constituted at Savannah, Ga. January 20, A.D. 1788: With Biographical Sketches of the Pastors. Philadelphia: J. Lippincott Co.

Skinner, Tom. 1975. If Christ is the Answer, What are the Questions? Grand Rapids: Zondervan Publishing House.

Smith, Gregory. 1980. The Ministry of Ushers. Collegeville, Minn.: Liturgical Press.

Smith, Theophus Harold. 1994. Conjuring Culture: Biblical Formations of Black America. New York: Oxford University Press.

Smitherman, Geneva. 1977. Talkin' and Testifyin': The Language of Black America. Boston: Houghton-Mifflin Co.

Sobel, Michael. 1979. Trabellin' On: The Slave Journey to an Afro-Baptist Faith. Westport, Conn.: Greenwood Press.

Southern, Eileen. 1971. The Music of Black Americans. New York: W. W. Norton.

Stack, Carol. 1974. All Our Kin: Strategies for Survival in a Black Community. New York: Harper & Row.

Stallings, J. O. 1988. Telling the Story: Evangelism in Black Churches. Valley Forge, PA: Judson Press.

Stevens, Abel. 1987. History of the Methodist Episcopal Church, Volume III, Book V.

Stuckey, Sterling. 1987. Slave Culture: Nationalist Theory and the Foundation of Black America. New York: Oxford Univ. Press.

Swartz, Sally. 1977. "First African Opens 187 Years of History." Savannah Morning News. Apr. 9.

Synan, Vinson. 1971. The Holiness Pentecostal Movement in the U.S. Grand Rapids, Michigan: Wm. B. Eerdmans.

Thomas, Edgar G. 1925. The First African Baptist Church of North America. Savannah: published by author.

Turner, Henry McNeal. 1971. Respect Black: The Writings and Speeches of Henry McNeal Turner. Comp. and ed. E. S. Redkey. New York: Arno Press.

Walker, Theodore. 1991. Empower the People: Social Ethics for the African-American Church. Maryknoll, NY: Orbis Books.

Walker, Wyatt Tee. 1979. "Somebody Calling My Name": Black Sacred Music and Social Change. Valley Forge, Pa.: Judson Press.

Wallace, James A. 1981. The Ministry of Lectors. Collegeville, Minn.: Liturgical Press.

Walters, R.W., and D.R. Brown. 1979. Exploring the Role of the Black Church in the Community. Washington, D.C.: Mental Health Research and and Development Center, Institute for Urban Affairs and Research, Howard University.

Waring, C. 1969. "History of the First Congregational Church." Mimeo. Georgia Historical Society.

Washington, Booker T. [1895] 1965. Up From Slavery. New York: Avon.

Waters, Ethel. 1951. His Eye Is on the Sparrow. Garden City, N.Y.: Doubleday.

Watson, Thomas J. 1917. Roman Catholics in America Falsifying History and Poisoning the Minds of Schoolchildren. Thompson, GA.: Jeffersonian Publishing Co.

Weisbrot, Robert. 1983. Father Divine and the Struggle for Racial Equality. Urbana: University of Illinois Press.

West, Cornel. 1982. Prophesy Deliverance. Philadelphia: Westminster.

White, Deborah. 1985. Ain't I a Woman: Female Slaves in the Plantation South. New York: W. W. Norton.

Wilkerson, Margaret B., and Jewell Handy Gresham. 1989. "The Racialization of Poverty." The Nation 249, no. 4 (July 24-31,1989): 126-32.

Williams, Raymond. 1958. Culture and Society, 1780-1950. New York: Doubleday.

Williamson, Joel. 1980. New People: Black/White Relations in the American South Since Emancipation. New York: Oxford Univ. Press.

Wilmore, Gayraud S. 1983. Black Religion and Black Radicalism. Maryknoll, N.Y.: Orbis Books.

Woodson, Carter. 1945. History of the Black Church. Washington: Associated.

# *INDEX*

# PRODUCT LISTING

**BOOKS - Community Economic Development**
❑    Community Economic Development: Challenges and Opportunities of Communities in Transition Workbook

**BOOKS - Education**
❑    Who Are We? Building A Knowledge Base About Different Ethnic, Racial and Cultural Groups in America (A Self-Paced Study and Facilitator's Guide)

**BOOKS - Religious**
❑    From the Garden of Eden to America
❑    The Study Guide for the Book of St. John (Knowing and Understanding Jesus Christ)
❑    Your Complete Study Guide on Salvation and the Holy Spirit

**MUSIC**
❑    Neda Hobbs - The Lady With A Song (cassette)

# ORDER FORM

**Type your name, shipping address and telephone number:**

Name

Company Name

Shipping Address

City

State/Province                                    ZIP/Postal Code

Daytime Phone (        )

(In case we have a question about your order)

**Please check your product choice here:**

| DESCRIPTION | QUANTITY | PRICE | TOTAL |
|---|---|---|---|
|  |  |  |  |
|  |  |  |  |
|  |  |  |  |
|  |  |  |  |
|  |  |  |  |

Calculate your total cost and indicate method of payment:

| | | |
|---|---|---|
| **Product Cost** | $ | **Payment method:** (See information listed below) |
| **US Sales Tax** | $ | **Check/money order** |
| **Freight** | $ | **Mastercard** |
| **Total Cost** | $ | **VISA** |

Distributed to the trade by:                        **Credit Card No.**

Associated Publishers Group
1501 County Hospital Road
Nashville, TN  37218                                **Expiration Date**
1-800-327-5713
e-mail:  cseneda@nmaa.org

**Cardholder's Signature**

## About the Author

*AVANEDA HOBBS, Ed.D., D.D.,* affectionately known as Lady Hobbs, is an accomplished educator, writer, preacher and vocalist.

THE LADY WITH A S[

Dr. Hobbs is sought after by many people, from all walks of life, because of her supernatural and God-given instincts for people's problems. She possesses an anointing to give incredible answers for almost unbelievable situations through love and profound biblical truths. Dr. Hobbs stirs many to faith and is known to provoke you to "take God at His Word and watch Him perform it -- He is our Divine Source." But, when you hear and see her, you'll surely get the idea that there can be more to faith than what we've experienced.

One of Dr. Hobbs' primary thrust, as an educator, is to instruct people on how to recognize, birth, understand the timing of a vision and the flowing into one's destiny. She spends a considerable amount of time educating people on the use of right perspectives as preventive medicine. She believes this serves as a means of setting the tone for productiveness and positive reinforcement.

Dr. Hobbs' experience as an educator was highlighted on a network syndicated television program, along with other well-known business professionals, to discuss the history and progression of black gospel music, christian music performance and public relations.

Dr. Hobbs' credits as a writer include books on the music industry, victorious christian living, community economic development, diversity and cultural awareness and several bible study guides.

As a vocalist, Lady Hobbs' musical artistry and statement reflects both a classical training and a strong pentecostal experience. Her vocal performances have been with and before senators, congressmen, mayors and several Grammy-award winning artists. Lady Hobbs has also been a featured vocalist on live album and videotaped recordings.